W9-BDH-563

How
to Be a
Doctor's Wife
without Really
Dying

# How
# to Be a
# Doctor's Wife
# without Really
# Dying

Second Edition

Marguerite Hurrey Wolf

Booklore Publishers, Inc.
Sarasota, Florida

ISBN 0-931110-00-9

*First Edition Copyright* © 1967 *by* Marguerite Hurrey Wolf
*Second Edition Copyright* © 1978 *by* Marguerite Hurrey Wolf

All rights reserved, including the right to reproduce this book or portions thereof in any form without permission of the copyright holder. For information address: Booklore Publishers, Inc., 785 North Osprey Avenue, Sarasota, Florida 33577.

*Library of Congress Catalog Card Number: 77-93115*

*Printed in the United States of America*

# *dedication*

To the two new men in George's and my life, Stephen Page and Patrick Strom, so that they may know what happened before they joined the family.

# preface

Let me say quickly that I make no claim to being a model doctor's wife. I've never kept his books, prepared the income tax return, boiled water for whatever you boil water for, or brought chicken soup to the laboratory at midnight. When my husband has asked for my help with a paper he has preferred his original draft. As a matter of fact, I assumed the role without any specific skills for a doctor's wife, no nerves of steel, no medical or nursing training, no independent income.

But I suppose that anyone who has the temerity to offer advice on how to sprout mung beans, construct a windmill, or how to be a doctor's wife without really dying is honor bound not only to present her credentials for posing as knowledgeable, but also to give some evidence of her success.

This is a treatise on survival, not success. But I have incontestable proof that the prognosis for survival is good. I'm alive, aren't I? Not only alive but in pretty good shape, or at least an unreasonable facsimile of the same shape I was in when I married into medicine. I tell myself, and anyone whose lapels I have firmly grasped in both hands, that I am the same woman my husband married. It just takes increasing amounts of time and money to look that way. And my experience has been varied. I have been the wife of five kinds of doctor—student, resident, board certified internist, medical college dean, and now professor of medicine—all the same man, you understand.

Of course every "How to" book starts with the assumption that you have the raw materials at hand. So I am assuming that you either have your medicine man bound, gagged, and swinging from the ridge pole, or that you have a bead on him and your scent is downwind. The chase is your problem. I'm just here to refute the widespread notion that the lot of a doctor's wife is a sorry one.

You don't have to agree with me. You don't even have to read the book. Feel free to use it to press violets or to balance the short leg of the card table. Or you may throw it at your husband's head. It's not weighty enough to hurt him physically and book throwing in moderation is indicated to improve the tone of any doctor's wife's psyche.

MARGUERITE HURREY WOLF

# acknowledgements

I wish to acknowledge my indebtedness to Mr. Edwin Géauque of Wake-Brook House, the publisher of the first edition of this book, for his permission to reprint in the present edition many of the chapters appearing in the first. I'm also indebted to the RESIDENT AND STAFF PHYSICIAN, TUFTS FOLIA MEDICA, and RISS MAGAZINE for their permission for use of certain chapters that appeared as articles in their publications.

And, of course, continuing thanks to George who got me into this whole delightful mess. I'm glad we started out in medicine when there were still heroes and no one was ashamed to revere them. And I'm equally glad that I can say after more than thirty years as a doctor's wife that I have always found the practice and teaching of medicine an honorable profession.

M. H. W.

# contents

# chapter 1

# What Doctor's Wife Would Dare Get Sick?

No sooner had I resumed my teaching job after the honeymoon than I awoke one morning with general malaise and a pain under my left ear. George, my husband, then a fourth-year student, was singing "Figaro" in the shower. I naturally expected him to leap solicitously to my side the instant I yelled my symptoms through the door. Instead he called back, "You old crock. Go on to school!"

I did and headed straight for the school doctor's office. The incumbent medico made his diagnosis before I was halfway to his desk. "You've got mumps!" he shouted. "Get out of here before you infect all the kids. Say, didn't you tell me your husband was almost through medical school?"

That's how I learned that, besides a sense of humor, a well-paying job, and a degree in business administration, the doctor's wife must be endowed with the knowledge of how to treat her own ailments till death do them part. She has a better chance of interesting her husband in the P.T.A. or the intricacies of making puff pastry than in her little old melanoma.

It is understandable that when said husband comes home from a hard day at the hospital he wants to get away from it all. But must he limit the contents of the medicine cabinet to shaving equipment, dental floss, bay rum, and a styptic pencil? His wife may be able to hide a small bottle of aspirin in the china closet, but he sees a thermometer as an unforgivable insult to his skill in the laying on of hands. His hand may be as sensitive as a radar antenna, but his wife gets only the back of it as far as healing is concerned.

When his wife is on the verge of collapse, he may break down and say indulgently, "I'll ask Tom to look at you." But if he should see Tom, and if Tom should happen to ask how his wife is, the answer probably would be, "She's fine."

When I became pregnant, four years after our marriage, I was used to having my symptoms ignored. So I almost fainted when George immediately signed me up for an appointment with the chief of obstetrics. I looked forward to asking the OB man all the questions I couldn't bother George with. But I was in and out of the office in exactly ten minutes, all but two of which were spent taking off and putting on my clothes.

The obstetrician did start to listen to my heart, but then he stopped, remarking, "Well, your husband knows more about that than I do." His nurse weighed me, assumed that I'd had routine blood tests at home, and gave me nothing except another appointment. I knew that having a baby was a perfectly natural, normal function. However, I couldn't help feeling a little smug when, after I finally got up the courage to insist on blood typing, I turned out to be an Rh-negative gravida.

It's well for the doctor's wife to espouse the cause of natural childbirth because that's what she's likely to have.

George was chief resident in medicine at the time our first child was born, and I wanted to make him proud of my behavior. I resolved not make a peep in the labor room. But as I lay there with only my small courage for company I realized that the baby was about to make his or her debut. I rang the bell. No answer. Why should there be? A doctor's wife is supposed to know how to take care of herself. I rang again. I shouted and waved to a passing nurse who waved back gaily and went on her way. Finally another nurse came along, took one look and bawled me out for not telling them that dilation was an understatement.

Several days later I told myself that I was glad I'd been perfectly conscious and unsedated throughout labor and delivery.

While it's hard for any doctor's wife to adjust to such apparent lack of concern for her comfort, the majority of us actually thrive on the treatment. I don't even get colds anymore. But there are a few doctors' wives who can't bear to let unwell enough alone. I'm going to visit one of them in the hospital today. She's a willing subject for the research, experiments, and theories of her husband and his colleagues. When her throat is scratchy it is sprayed with one hand and cultured with the other. Between urinalyses, spinal taps, and smears, she has hardly a cell to call her own. I'm not planning to take her anything because she already has everything—ruptured discs, postnasal drip, menopausal syndrome (she's twenty-nine), and, of course, depression. The only diseases she doesn't have are those that are limited to organs she's already had taken out. Her vision is too blurred to read the handwriting on the wall of the O.R., but I can read it even though my eyes haven't been tested for fifteen years.

'Tis said that the doctor's opinion shouldn't be questioned. So when George tells me I'm healthy I guess I am. Even though I'm not always convinced I've learned not to argue. Whenever I forget myself and start complaining George casually comments, "If I'd wanted a patient at home I'd have married one."

So my advice to medical brides is this: Buy a box of Band-Aids and a first-aid book, learn to reduce your own fractured ego, and be prepared to drive yourself to the hospital when the pains get five minutes apart.

## chapter  2

# The Lean Years
# Become the
# Good Old Days

I can't remember whether it was six or seven years in the Bible, but it is approximately the same number of lean years faced by every resident physician and his wife if they marry during medical school days. It isn't only "Yond Cassius" who has "a lean and hungry look," it's young Dr. Kildare and all the rest who can't save anything but wear and tear on their civilian clothes while they are men in white.

When George and I were married, all but two of those present thought it was a terrible idea. Our parents sniffled and smiled bravely through the brief ceremony as though it were a wake. George's fellow students looked upon it as a sort of youthful folly although we were both twenty-five years old. When he applied for an internship, several professors warned George that being married was a definite liability. "After all," one remarked, "we don't want a house officer who goes out dancing every night."

Of course the married medical student is now the norm. It is the bachelor, the poor but honest, or rich and wary student who is the odd ball. This was brought home to us quite literally the first year that George was dean of the University of Vermont College of Medicine. We asked all the students' wives out to our farm for a chance to get acquainted with these "lonely" girls. Lonely, my foot! They arrived in clutches, complete with one, two, and even three children apiece. At that time, fortunately, we had ninety acres, a gamboling white lamb, ducklings, five sheep, kittens, and two young daughters who acted as hostesses. The place swarmed with what seemed like twice as many wives as there were enrolled students, and even more children. When George and I were married there were two other married students in his class of eighty.

But back to "the olden days," as our daughters put it so callously. I'd love to be able to tell an inspiring tale of sacrifice and hardship but it just wasn't that way. True we had little money but what we had was very elastic. Food bills, eight dollars a week; rent, fifty dollars a month. We had no car, no children, no insurance, no equity, but neither did anyone else whom we knew. Liquor was party fare, not a household staple. George had a small research fellowship, and I mean *small* in terms of those days. I was paid $1500 a year as a teacher.

Never since have we been so rich. The first Christmas George gave me a Hamilton watch that's still running and I gave him a movie projector, which also would run if I weren't too lazy to take it out and use it. We lived high on the hog even though no one was bringing home much bacon. Of course we had one big advantage over the present medical students. We were just emerging from the depression and we hadn't grown accustomed to the face of affluence. Jobs were scarce and not to be treated lightly. I worked as a clinic aide one summer (teachers have long vacations) five and a half days a week for $18 per week. I felt lucky to get the job. We didn't miss the cars we had never owned. Babies were not considered the immediate sequel to marriage. We not so naively planned to have children when we could afford them, and did.

All students' wives who did not have children worked. They taught school, did research, or were secretaries according to training and talents.

Contrary to the popular myth, I don't think that any of the group I knew put their husbands through medical school. The boys either had a fellowship or a loan or a father to pay their tuition, and the girls maintained the household. Our apartments were furnished from our parents' attics, Macy's basement, and wedding presents.

When George was on the house staff we lived in an elderly apartment house across the street from New York Hospital. We called it Cockroach Hall for reasons that were obvious after dark, but cockroaches weren't the only specialty of the house. In addition to the figurative wolf at the door we had very real silverfish, moths, and many, many mice.

The dominating articles of furniture in our living-dining-cooking room were an oversized couch and armchair that George's parents had been happy to part with. This furniture was twenty years old when we inherited it. After serving as trains, ferry boats, and cowboy ponies for small fry in its original home and experiencing constant use by the adult population of Cockroach Hall it was showing its age.

7

The springs of the chair gave a weary sigh and sank down to the floor. George, being an inveterate do-it-yourselfer, decided that he was as bright as the average upholsterer, bought himself cord and canvas and lethal-looking needles, took the chair apart, and retied the springs. I'm sure that he was right about being as bright but he was less well endowed with practice and patience. It took him fifteen long evenings to complete the job and he has never argued an uphosterer's bill since. After he got the springs tied he borrowed a second-hand sewing machine from a pretty little student's wife who lived downstairs and across the hall. The sight of George hunched over that machine, stuffing its unwilling mouth with heavy fabric, gave me qualms of guilt but not severe enough to overcome my dread of the contraption.

For the couch, George decided that euthanasia was a kinder fate than torturing it with his needles and knots. So when we were about to move to a new apartment, just completed on the site of the old gas tanks at York Avenue and Sixty-third Street, we planned to part with Big Red, our dinosaur davenport. I called a second-hand man who made his opinion clear with, "Listen, lady, holes in my head I haven't got. Oy vay! I got troubles enough already."

I called the Goodwill Industries and they sent around a truck and two men. The truck was mercifully silent but the two men lectured me on the waste of their time and gas, and chided me about my insulting offer until the couch and I were nearly reduced to tears.

We decided that we would just haul Big Red out onto the sidewalk and let the Sanitation Department take over. Foiled again. Our "super" told us they would refuse to take it and we would have to pay someone to have it carted off to some potter's field for destitute furniture.

George was regaling the director of the hospital with the sad tale when, to his astonishment, this gentleman said that he would be glad to send men and a dolly to pick up Big Red if we would just sign a paper giving it to New York Hospital. It would be repaired in the hospital shop and used in one of the lounges. But Big Red had one glorious moment of retribution! On the day of its removal George was walking into the main entrance of the hospital with a group of trustees and department heads. Under the very noses of this august gathering, Big Red was carried in with all the t.l.c. accorded to a patient in cardiac failure. There were smiles and raised eyebrows on the faces of all but that of rosy-visaged George.

About a year later we were at a party in the house staff lounge on the eighteenth floor. Suddenly George nudged my elbow and whispered, "Don't look now, but isn't that leather-covered couch someone we know?" Big Red had come into its own and for all I know still cradles the nether portions of the physicians of the future.

At the same sort of gathering in Kansas City, two medical students were objecting to the pigeon-holing of students. The students objected but I could tell from the smiles on the faces of their wives that these women thought their pigeons fitted.

For instance: True or False?

First-year students are starry-eyed and plan to become general practioners. They are impressed with themselves for getting into medical school and they are going to alleviate the miseries of mankind. *Student's answer:* False. *Student's wife's answer:* True.

Second-year students are always sick. The etiology of these illnesses starts with the words in medical textbooks, proceeds from the brain to the organs involved and produces sweating, anxiety, anorexia nervosa as well as typical disease symptoms. *Student's answer:* False. *Student's wife's answer:* True.

Third-year students have miraculously developed immunity to most disorders but have changed their goals from general practice to a specialty. *Student's answer:* True, with lengthy explanation. *Student's wife's answer:* True, with lengthy sigh caused by realization that the vine-covered cottage has just gone over the hill for a few more years.

Fourth-year students are preoccupied with applications for internships. They spend most of their non-working hours in bull sessions about the merits of rotating internships, specialty training, the comparative financial security of the armed forces, and the diminishing astuteness of the attendings. Fourth-year students are always tired. *Student's answer:* None. Too busy talking. *Student's wife's answer:* When do we pack?

Time may have changed some of these categories but I'll never forget the way George's classmates fell asleep during their fourth year. George didn't fall asleep but he and I gave up trying to impress each other by walking miles through art museums or standing through an entire opera just below the ceiling. We were both too tired to stand up and when it became painfully evident that we'd be more comfortable sitting on Big Red than cross-legged on the hard bare floor of the peanut gallery at the old Metropolitan Opera House, we voted for comfort rather than culture.

George wasn't the only tired one. It took all the hoarse cacophony of the German-American beer hall to keep his classmates awake.

One evening Ken MacDonald, best man at our wedding, came over to Cockroach Hall to have dinner with us. Ken's eating procedure reminded me of a raccoon, except he didn't dip everything in

*"Ken never stirred."*

water. After carefully eating all of his broccoli, then all of his mashed potatoes, then cutting his meat into tiny pieces and chewing it thoughtfully, he dragged himself three feet across the room where he collapsed on Big Red and promptly fell asleep. I washed the dishes, George turned on the radio. We talked and read until eleven, made ourselves a sandwich, rustled the newspapers, stuck a pillow under Ken's head, and still Ken slept on. With a sudden inspiration, George stuck an artificial lily in Ken's hand, folded his arms in a prayerful attitude, got out flash bulbs, and took a picture for posterity. Ken never stirred. We placed a glass of milk and a sandwich beside him and went to bed.

In the morning the plate, the glass, and Big Red were empty. Sometime before dawn Ken had roused sufficiently to return to his furnished room on Sixty-eighth Street. Such was standard procedure. The only unusual feature was that we had recorded the typical comatose condition of a fourth-year student.

And then came the day of caps and gowns, parents blocking traffic on York Avenue, the Hippocratic Oath, and a confusion of goodbyes. It didn't seem possible. It was almost a letdown until we crossed the street, and came back home to Cockroach Hall where we met Carl, our faithful if garlic-flavored doorman, beaming in the hall. "Nice day, DOCTOR," he said and shook George's hand.

Oh, the good old days at Cockroach Hall! They were the lean years, but . . . ! Everyone in the building was in the same boat, a leaky one financially. What we lacked in luxury we made up in laughs.

Barbara and Clarke lived in the apartment below us. Barbara was very young, very pretty, and preferred her man to a mouse. Early one evening she catapulted through our door, wild-eyed, barefoot, and clad in a nightgown.

"There's a mouse down there," she gasped, "and Clarke's on tonight."

Ever ready to help a damsel in distress, especially a pretty one, George left his spaghetti and charged downstairs to the rescue, with Barbara following at a safe distance. While Barbara leaped from one chair to another, pointing and shrieking, George managed to murder the mouse under the bed. Just as George was squirming out from under the bed, and Barbara was in the middle of one of her leaps, Clarke walked in. Clarke's strong voice, sonorous then as now, bellowed out across the fire escapes, rattling windows for blocks. Many tenants, who are now deans, professors, or practitioners, will never forget that blast.

"What the hell are you doing chasing my wife around in her nightgown?" Clarke screamed.

George, dusty and red-faced from exertion, staggered to his feet and, holding the dead mouse gingerly by the tail and thrusting it at Clarke, announced icily, "HERE is what I was chasing, and as for the nightgown, doesn't your wife own a dress?"

Aware of his error but sensitive to the slur on his wife's wardrobe, Clarke quietly and with irrefutable logic replied, "She owns one but it's got to last three years, and slips and nightgowns are cheaper, you fathead."

Clarke is now Chairman of the Board of a large drug company. When he and Barbara flew East

*13*

a few years ago George and I met them in front of their hotel in Cambridge. As we approached, Barbara calmly shed her mink stole, handed it to George, and wordlessly turned slowly around in front of him, displaying a very new, well-cut wool dress.

Once when my parents sent us a basket of grapefruit from Florida, I rushed downstairs with a skirtful of the fruit to share our largesse. When George came home he looked at the half-empty basket, walked over near the heating pipes leading to the floor below and shouted, "I suppose you gave half of these to Barbara." Moments later grapefruit began rolling through our open door followed by Clarke's voice, "Keep your Indian River fruit, you Indian giver. We're perfectly happy with our ascorbic acid samples."

Meanwhile George added to his reputation as a man among mice when Margaret, from the floor above us, phoned in tears.

"Dan's on admitting. I've caught a mouse but I can't move."

"Why not?" George wanted to know.

"Because I'm sitting on it."

Sure enough, Margaret, with the phone on her lap, was sitting on a wastebasket, trapping the mouse therein. In a message on a Christmas card received some years latter, Dan wrote, "Margaret now sits on speakers' platforms and school boards. She much prefers them to mice."

Kay was our only female neighbor who not only tolerated mice but worked with them, white ones. She and her husband, Tom, are both M.D.s. She was not fazed by vermin or ventricles but she locked and bolted the apartment door to bar sales-

14

men or other unwanted intruders. When George wished to discuss a case with Tom he had to scream his identity through the door before Kay would unjangle it with maneuvers like those required to open Jack Benny's vault. One night George pulled on a hideous rubber mask, a grotesque Boris Karloff number that covered his entire head and neck, shrugged his overcoat collar up around Mr. Karloff's ears, and sallied forth to educate Kay. Kay wasn't educated. George was.

The human residents of Cockroach Hall shared recipes, windfalls, and children. It was a wise child at 1303 York Avenue who knew his own father. Any man in white was "Daddy," which embarrassed our bachelor friends so much that they soon married to preserve their honor.

We were poor but everyone else was too. Well, not everyone. There was one intern with inherited money who had a penthouse, cook, and governess for his two children. We felt a little sorry for him and his wife. They couldn't raid the icebox, take off their shoes, or scream at each other. They were strangers in their penthouse paradise. Their marriage broke up soon after graduation. The rest of us never contemplated divorce. We were too busy, too much in love, too honorable, and much too poor. If those were the lean years, I'll bet on the lean horse for a long race.

Though we scattered to Oregon, Kansas, and Vermont, we still see each other, often when our children are crisscrossing the continent to college. The kids, sicklied o'er with the current pale cast of uninvolvement, are wide-eyed at the warmth of these reunions. When we roll back the years and the rugs,

we end up rolling with laughter. We had plenty of
nothing but nothing must have been plenty for us.
The house-staff years leaned heavily on the staff of
life, learning, laughter, and love.

# chapter 3

# Should She Go to Medical Meetings?

Someone once said that you are crazy if you drink before you are forty and crazy if you don't after you pass that milestone. The same thing is true for wives tagging along to medical meetings. But doctors' wives seem to have dual birthplaces—one, the spot where they first saw the light of day, and, two, Missouri. You can't tell them anything. They have to find out for themselves the hard way.

I'll never forget my first and last A.M.A. meeting in Atlantic City. Several of us were planning to drive down from New York together. The thought of this rare outing, the chance to spend two days with our husbands at the shore in May, had sent Barbara and me into a twister of plans. We scurried around assembling adequate wardrobes, no mean task in my case because I was four months pregnant, too bulgy for my regular clothes and not enceinte enough to be willing to wear the two saggy tents leftover from my first pregnancy. But nothing could dim our enthusiasm. I would have worn a grain bag, and probably looked as though I had.

We would have breakfast in bed. We would window-shop, since any other kind of shopping was out of the question. We would spend long hours anointing ourselves for the cocktail hour to be followed by fascinating little dinners with our husbands. We would sleep through two nights without hearing, "Mommy, Iwantadrinkawater" or that miserable telephone. We would eat food we hadn't cooked ourselves and it wouldn't be Jell-O or "pasquetti" either. We could hardly wait.

We did all of those things planned but there was one thing lacking. It was what is always lacking at medical meetings, our husbands. From the moment our mates fell out of the car and onto their confreres' necks with shouts of recognition and rehashes of gallbladders, pneumothoraces, and eclampsia, we were the forgotten women.

Ruth, another doctor's wife, who was an old hand at such things was undaunted. "Come on," she said. "This is all going to be fecaliths in the pericardium or Ritter's tisny. It's every woman for herself."

"By herself" would have been more precise. The men slipped out of bed at dawn to get to the breakfast meetings at seven-thirty. If we happened to bump into them outside of the crowded meeting rooms they slipped us some money for lunch and promised to re-establish contact before dinner. We exhausted the pleasures of the boardwalk in one morning. It was too cold to sit on the beach and too crowded to sit anywhere else. I was so excited when the husbands really did appear at five and offered to buy us a drink that I gulped down one of those famous lethal punches that taste like grandma's raspberry shrub but hit you like a Mickey Finn. I naively asked a professor of medicine if his wife had come and he laughingly replied, "Heavens, no. She came once, years ago. We prefer to take our vacations together." This didn't make much sense to me at the time but I blamed it on the punch.

We all talked until Barbara and I began to realize that the only one who listened to either of us was one of us two. So we smiled and waited. We smiled and waited until eight o'clock when someone began to mention dinner. We smiled and waited another hour while the husbands rounded up good old Tom Endocrinology and Eckleberry Metabolism. My own metabolism was occupying my attention. Even if anyone had spoken to me I wouldn't have dared answer. The witches' brew that looked so inoffensive had left me just this side of drunk. I was having trouble focusing my eyes, let alone my attention.

Finally thirty of us got into five taxis and we hurtled to Hackneys for lobster. There we waited and smiled another hour while the head waiter smiled and kept us waiting. When we finally got to the tables I was so delighted to sit down that I nearly fell asleep. Somehow the idea of lobster was no longer so appealing, but my feeble protests were shouted down. When my rosy, glistening lobster stared up at me glassily, I stared back at him with visage equally pink, glistening and glassy-eyed. We were both boiled and hors de combat. As a wave of nausea swept over me I retired unsteadily to the ladies' room where I waited and smiled wanly at the sad-eyed attendant until our delegation had cracked the last claw and swabbed up the last bit of congealed drawn butter. Back at the hotel, I spent most of the night flicking our bathroom light on and off while experiencing my first case of Atlantic City crud.

By the time we were on our way home I felt fine. I couldn't wait to get home so that I could talk to George.

Later on, however, when our children were older and George was traveling a great deal, I took to the road with him and we both enjoyed it. Not only did my presence provide George with a companion, a sounding board, and an excuse not to be dragged around to the overpriced and under-talented night spots that a few of his colleagues still thought they relished, but it provided him with a shirt-and-sock-washer as well. By that time we both knew so many of the medical school deans and administrators so well that these meetings were reunions with friends whom we enjoyed. We went to Denver, Miami, San Francisco, New Orleans, Hawaii, and Puerto Rico. George still had breakfast meetings, luncheon meetings, and all-day meetings, but we sneaked off to dinner together to eateries that I believed to be only names in GOURMET magazine—Brennan's, Top o' the Mark, and Bookbinders. Twice we went a day ahead, rented a car, and played golf. Between meetings we caught a quick swim. And I learned that wives become the privileged ones instead of the neglected ones. The hostesses in each city take the visiting fireladies on wonderful tours, up into the Rockies, through historic mansions or over the cobbled streets of the Vieux Carré.

The 1965 meetings of the A.A.M.C. were something I wouldn't have believed twenty-five years ago. George was the outgoing president and we were given the presidential suite at the Sheraton Hotel in Philadelphia—not at our expense, you understand; the hotels throw in these suites that they have little call for along with the arrangements for hundreds of reservations. There was even a gleaming brass plaque on the door proclaiming "Presidential Suite." As we followed the bellman down the mile of red carpet towards this shining beacon, I kept thinking "a title on the door rates a Bigelow on the floor." I also kept tapping my fingers against every other door we passed. It's an invaluable trick I've learned over the years. At least it is invaluable to me. If you like to have an electric shock nearly knock the key out of your hand, don't do it; just scuff along those long carpeted corridors and crackle and snap at the end. But, if you play tick-tack on the doors as you go along, presto, no shock when you reach your little home away from home.

Our suite had flowers, Scotch, salted nuts, an enormous drawing room, two bedrooms, two bathrooms, a den with its own powder room which I used for the laundry, a formal dining room, and a rattly sort of a kitchenette. The drawing room had a few valuable Eighteenth Century antiques with plaques on them telling how valuable. There was an ornate painted television set. There were massive walnut secretaries and a few life-sized plaster Dianas and Mercuries about to take off. I tentatively pulled the drawer handle on one highboy hoping to find a piece of writing paper, a postcard, or even a laundry list. No writing materials, but the drawer pull came off in my hand. I guiltily hid it in the empty drawer.

The suite also had four telephones. The incoming president and his wife, Lorna and Tommy Turner, from Johns Hopkins, had moved into one of the bedrooms, but I didn't know this the first day. Their bedroom opened into the hall as well as into

*21*

the drawing room. When a call came for either of the men, only the pink phone on the console next to the marble fireplace in the drawing room rang. This I had to find out the hard way. I heard a phone ring as I was stepping out of the shower. I put one arm in my robe and picked up the white phone in our bedroom. No sound. I trotted into the den and picked up the beige phone. No sound. Struggling to get my

*"Sure enough, a voice!"*

damp arms into my robe, I ran through the kitchen-ette, around the huge dining-room table, into the vast reaches of the drawing room, and slid to a halt at the pink phone next to the marble mantle. Sure enough, a voice! A reporter from one of the Philadelphia papers. I was still struggling with the bathrobe cord, the phone cord, and two sleeves much like Laocoön and his sons struggled with the sea serpents, and the serpents were winning.

It wasn't until the next day that a couple of awful thoughts struck me. What if Tommy Turner had catapulted out of the bedroom on the right as I made my entrance from the left in the not-quite-alto-gether? What if I had charged in there, myopic and damply deshabille, while one of the endless commit-tee meetings had been in progress? Of course I know this group pretty well, but I require more than my bathrobe cord and one sleeve to look my best.

I've learned some tricks over the years of attending medical meetings. Here are some recom-mendations. Take low-heeled shoes for walking. If you have to stand in a receiving line, or just plain stand, change your shoes half way through the mar-athon. If you travel by plane, put any spray can that you need in carry-on luggage because the can might part with its contents if in a suitcase in the unpres-surized baggage area. Anyway, spray cans may soon be outlawed. November or December meetings pro-vide an opportunity to "write" Christmas cards, so, at this time of year, take the cards along. Take your address book so that you may write to all those people you've been putting off writing to. Take a bathing cap if the meeting is in Florida because get-ting into a pool without one is forbidden and who

23

wants to spend nine dollars for a flowery, rubber hornets' nest when one has a perfectly good simpler model at home? Also take green make-up base to camouflage your sunburned nose into a semblance of human flesh. Always take a bottle opener, for obvious reasons. You'll use a folding rainbonnet as often as your toothbrush, unfortunately; and don't forget spot remover for the stain left by the chicken gravy that the waiter always pours down your back at banquets. You won't need half the clothes you take but you can't be sure which half to leave behind. A wig would be great in Miami, but, on me, wigs never look as good as they do in the advertisements.

In the house-staff years, going to medical meetings or not going to medical meetings really boils down to whether or not you want out so badly that your sanity is in question. If going will preserve sanity, go by all means. It's cheaper than a psychiatrist but remember that a psychiatrist will give you the undivided attention you'll never get at a medical meeting.

## chapter 4

# Hear No Evil, Speak No Evil

When I was a mere slip of an intern's wife, and probably clad only in a slip to save my working clothes, an older doctor's wife stopped in to offer me some advice.

"What a young doctor's wife needs to learn is how to keep quiet in two languages, English and Medicine."

I laughed politely because, of course, I knew I would never gossip about George's patients. I wouldn't, eh? Less than two years later I had to learn the hard way.

One evening George described to me the bizarre behavior of a pretty young patient who flung off her white gown and pranced up and down in the altogether. He prudently withheld her name, but sometime later, at a gathering of house officers and their wives, I thought of the incident and regaled the group with a bounce-by-bounce account. Too late I saw George's agonized face and frantic gestures. The lady involved was at my elbow and she wasn't laughing. She was frozen silent.

Later George was very vocal and the text of his sermon was from Uncle Remus, "Tar Baby, he say nuthin'." That was made easy for a long time because Tar Baby was told nothing until she learned to button her lip. Just as well. If you see no evil and hear no evil, it is not hard to emulate the third monkey and speak no evil.

The danger lies not simply in embarrassment to you, your husband, and the patient, but in the false implication that a casual remark may convey. The knowledge of malignancy, alcoholism, or mental illness may even change your attitude from natural warmth to solicitous or elaborately casual behavior. The patient goes to your husband in confidence and the destruction of this confidence not only may aggravate his problem but can jeopardize the doctor's ability to help the patient.

If you work in his office or send out the bills, or even answer the phone at home, you will inevitably know who some of your husband's patients are. But it is none of your business WHY they are his patients. The patient has the right to put on his privacy as well as his clothing at the end of his appointment with the doctor. Put yourself in the patient's place. If you have a mole that turns out not to be a melanoma, or a husband who goes overboard with another woman and then realizes (with a little help from you) that he'd rather pull his oar in your lifeboat, wouldn't you prefer that only your doctor, instead of the hairdresser, knew for sure?

Of course a doctor's wife can't be totally silent on the phone. But beyond "hello" the role is largely one of taking down the name, phone number, and relevant information. After all, the voice the patient would like to hear is not your own.

If, however, your husband sleeps soundly

at night, with a protective deafness to the phone, give him several moments to struggle out of the clutches of Morpheus and mobilize his wits. Once, in the middle of the night, the daughter of an elderly patient called to tell George that her mother had just died. I handed the phone to my drowsy partner who propped himself up on one elbow.

"Mother's gone," the daughter whispered sadly.

"Gone!" George exclaimed. "In her condition? Where's she gone?"

Hit the snoozing gent on the head with a pillow. Throw cold water in his face, if you don't mind changing the bedding. Walk him around the room twice, do anything, but be sure he's back from the Land of Nod before he picks up the phone.

When George was resident in medicine at New York Hospital, one of the assistant residents could do a perfect imitation of the Professor of Medicine. The professor had great dignity, a deep resonant voice, and wavy white hair. One evening our phone rang when George was on call. When an impressive bass voice rolled over the wire intoning, "Marguerite, this is David Barr; I need to reach George at once," I was sure that it was Dan Labby and not our revered mentor.

I snorted with glee and cracked back, "Why, Uncle David, with that voice you could reach him anywhere."

There was a long silence, followed by, "I'm sorry but this IS Dr. Barr."

I was sorrier than he. I still wince at the memory though he would be the first to laugh about it now.

Listen to records in Hindi. Be fluent in Mandarin, but you'll earn your husband's respect when you become dumb in Medicine.

The reason that deans' wives stay limber is that they get a lot of exercise practicing how to keep their feet out of their mouths. Within the first week of my tenure as deaness I had to extricate my size eight-and-a-half foot from my equally outsized mouth twice.

Our furniture was still in storage when there were dedication ceremonies for new wings of the Mary Fletcher Hospital, and the trustees gave a large reception. I had met none of the trustees or their wives and few of the medical faculty. So I thought I should bone up a little on who the trustees were, their names, occupations, and previous condition of servitude. Being prone to blocking on names under stress, even that of my college roommate, I prepared a little dossier: Mr. D., investment broker and conservation enthusiast; Mr. S., banker, old Burlington family, uncle of a friend of mine; Mr. P., granite memorials and other enterprises, big white house; Mr. T., insurance executive. That sort of thing.

I was rather proud of my little homemade Who's Who, and thought I had memorized it. I had. But there is such a thing as over-studying. You don't become stale; you become stupid. As I sailed down the line I linked up faces with notes, murmuring under my breath, "S stands for Savings Bank." But a few minutes later I was called upon to introduce a new faculty member to the wife of one of the trustees who owned a large cereal factory in Burlington. My memory served but I got the occupation before the appellation and heard myself say, "Dr. X., I'd like you to meet Mrs. Maltex."

The next evening there was a formal dinner and, not owning an evening gown of more recent vintage than bridesmaids' dresses, I whisked down to a local store and bought a black velvet top and a black and white cut-velvet skirt. I felt quite chic and swept confidently across the room to meet the other deans and their wives. The first lady and I stared at each other in fascination and then burst out laughing. We were dressed exactly alike!

Then there was the problem of house-hunting in a town as closely knit as Burlington. We were fresh from the impersonal towers of Manhattan and it never occurred to me that half the population in Burlington knew what houses were on the market, their approximate values, and who had lived in them. I was gaily telling one colleague's wife about the monstrosity that I had visited that day, describing its ugly woodwork, antiquated kitchen, and exorbitant price. I thought she cooled perceptibly and I asked her if she knew the house.

"Every newel post," she replied; "that's my family homestead."

The children too had to be trained that folkways vary with the folk. In Jericho, where we had spent four summers before we moved to Burlington, spiritual matters were in the capable hands of two lady ministers. I helped with their daily Vacation Bible School and we became friends. One day I invited these ladies to lunch at our house. Patty, aged five, was helping as waitress. For drinking purposes we preferred the water from our hillside spring to that of the well under the summer kitchen, so we kept spring water in two large liquor bottles in the refrigerator. It was a hot day and I asked Patty to refill our water glasses. Her small voice carried out from the kitchen, "Which bottle, Mommy, the gin bottle or the whisky bottle?"

The lady ministers had their revenge a few days later when they unexpectedly stopped by and asked to see our brook and natural swimming pool down in the woods behind the house. George, hot and dirty from rototilling the garden, had run down to the pool, pulled off his clothes, soaped himself, and plunged into the icy water to rinse off. Down the path came the two visitors, calling out gaily to George, whose face turned red. They loved the pool. They sat down on a log and chatted. George's face gradually turned from red to blue as he trod water, immersed to the neck in the deepest and farthest corner of the pool. "My," they commented, when I finally lured them back up to the house, "what endurance he must have to stay in that cold water so long!"

Over the years in South Burlington our two little girls became very adept at passing drinks and hors d'oeuvres. The department heads came so often to our house for cocktail parties to meet prospective faculty members that Patty and Debbie called them "The Boys' Club." They knew each man's preference in liquor and food. One day, seven-year-old Debbie, posted as lookout at the window, called to her father, the bartender, "Here come one martini, one very weak manhattan, and a couple of whisky and branch waters."

At first I assumed that all the doctors in Vermont knew each other and that I was the only unknown quantity. Often there was no need for introductions. But when I saw one man stand at the edge of a group rather awkwardly and then intro-

*"Here come one martini, one very weak manhattan, and a couple of whisky and branch waters."*

duce himself, I resolved to tighten up my role as hostess.

I made a point of introducing everyone, racking my brain to remember names or slipping into the kitchen for a quick consultation with George. It was hard to match up several hundred names and faces in the first few weeks, but I tried. Then one day the head of pediatrics and his wife came to our house. Good. I knew them, Jim and Liz

McKay. Then in came Ethan and Doro Sims. What luck! We lived across the meadow from them. I proudly introduced Doro to Liz; both formally acknowledged the introduction, grinning from ear to ear. What was so funny? I knew their names but I was derelict in my genealogy. They were first cousins!

After several years a dean's wife acquires tricks to compensate for the gaps in her memory. If I see someone approaching and block on the name, I now calmly say, "Of course you know my husband, George Wolf," and I don't mention the unknown name at all. Or I say, "Do you know each other?" and then before they answer I drift off to greet a newcomer. It's sneaky and if it weren't for the blessing of those name tags on most of the delegates at medical meetings I'd never get away with it. But the gimmicks fail you sometimes. I once heard a hostess ask, "How do you spell your name?" And the guest obliged by spelling it out. I tucked this away in my bag of tricks for future use. A while later I thought I had the right moment to camouflage the fact that a dimly familiar face, bearing down upon a desk where I was helping to make out the name tags, was nameless.

"Do you spell your name with an i or an e?" I asked, hoping that the deaness next to me would recognize him.

"Which do YOU think?" he countered. "I'm Bob Hill."

*chapter* 5

# "Who's Lonely?"
# She Sobbed

I've spent a lot of time with the wives of interns and residents over the last thirty years and for three years before that I was such a wife myself. Unlike the man imagining a purple cow, I'd rather be than see one. I loved our residency years for two reasons. George was having such an exciting time that his enthusiasm was contagious, and I had no preconceived notion that the life of a doctor's wife was one of luxury.

If I have learned anything from the chuckles, sobs, panel discussions, and gripes over the years it is that the unhappy wife is haunted by an image of herself as "the doctor's wife." When reality doesn't match this image, and it rarely does, she wails like a banshee or becomes resentful and hypochondriacal.

Everyone talks about image so much these days that, like any word repeated many times in succession, it has lost its meaning. We've forgotten that it is related to the word imagination, that it is something thought up and invented, not the real thing.

If the real doctor's wife will please stand up you will see that she isn't an image. She's alive. She is the girl the medical student or intern married not because she was beautiful, intelligent, or had a good job, although she may be endowed with all of these, but because he wanted to spend his life with her.

Some house-staff wives pictured the doctor's wife as a leader, a person with status in the community, living in a large house with wall-to-wall carpeting, two new cars in the garage, and a mink stole in her closet.

If that's your image, forget it. You are doomed to chronic unhappiness until you realize that cars and carpeting are not antidotes for that condition. There is nothing wrong with being a social leader if you think of society as including everyone. There is nothing wrong with carpeting or new cars or mink stoles but they don't do a thing for your personality. Look at some of the old girls at Miami Beach hardly able to totter after their poodles because of the weight of their wigs, jewels, and furs. Have these accoutrements improved their image? Do their faces radiate serenity and inner peace?

The doctors' wives who are happy live in the present, and the present during the house-staff years means very little money and very little time with a husband who gets very little sleep. Of course you are lonely some of the time and of course you are poor most of the time. You can't entirely eliminate either of these problems but there are lots of things you can do to improve them or to make them more tolerable.

One is to make your friends among other house officers and their wives so that you don't compare your life to that of other couples who have more money and more time to spend together. Try to live

34

near some other residents so that you can pool your meager resources. You can baby-sit for each other, plan suppers together rather than yearn to go out, and swap recipes, records, books, and anything but husbands and wives.

If you are working, try to find a job that you like, at least a little, even if it brings in less money than one you don't like. You aren't likely to find a dream job, but if you don't absolutely hate the one you have, you won't feel sorry for yourself. Why shouldn't you be an earning partner during these years? Your husband is going to be supporting you for the rest of your life. This is a cooperative enterprise isn't it? Or do you expect to be maintained in the fashion to which either Daddy or the magazines have accustomed you? You may have been born with a silver spoon in your mouth but now it's a tongue depressor and the best way to keep from gagging on a tongue depressor is to relax and breathe through your mouth.

If you are lonely, use this solitude to learn something new. Every skill, new word, and recipe that you learn you will use. They will widen your world and also your understanding of it. I never scream at telephone operators because I once was one and became so nervous when I disconnected important long distance calls that my hands got wet and I got electric shocks from the metal plugs.

Continue your education while your husband is continuing his, by reading—newspapers, classics, best sellers—everything except movie magazines and his medical books. The movie magazines won't develop anything but your hip measurements and his medical books will develop your imagination in the wrong way. Libraries are free. Many lectures are free and so are most museums.

And, finally, watch out for the most common pitfall of all. When you think that your husband pays more attention to his patients than he does to you, don't become a patient to get his attention. You may think he is only interested in symptoms, but he's not interested in hearing about yours. He hears complaints and symptoms all day and most nights. What he really yearns for is the sight of a healthy, cheerful face on the front of an alert mind, preferably yours.

*chapter* 6

# The Doctor and a New Suit: An Allergic Reaction

Why is it that every doctor worth his monosodium glutamate considers shopping for a new suit in the same category as having a tooth extracted? And for the same reasons: because it is painful, undignified, and takes time and money. No one near or dear to the victim should have to watch this traumatic scene. Like primitive male tribal rites it should be kept hidden from female eyes. But the truth is that no doctor of my acquaintance would set foot inside a men's clothing emporium, be it Barney's or Brooks Brothers, if he wasn't dragged along the pavement, scratching and trying to dig in all the way, by the little woman.

In the first place he apparently is pretty ashamed that he is finally protruding out of those two suits he bought two or was it three years ago? This harks back to his childhood when he was scolded for ripping his pants shinnying up the shagbark hickory tree or taking the short cut over that nail on the back fence. From the moment he is propelled into the haberdashery drooping in the shoulders and with adhesive feet, it is a contest in non-communication between the doctor and the salesman. This is standard procedure from the male point of view but one of life's mysteries to me on the sidelines. Men's clothing salesmen are coached in rules of the game and consider it a point of honor not to acknowledge the customer's presence for a decent interval. So the salesman makes a show of looking in several directions, busies himself with invisible fragments of lint on his left trouser leg, and examines his right lower molar in the nearest mirror.

After these first feinting maneuvers the salesman puts on his hearty "Well, well, what have we here?" smile and addresses me, not my husband, George, with a rhetorical, "Is there anything in a suit that we could show you today?"

Well, the only things IN a suit are George in his rump-sprung shiny old set of threads and the salesman in his poured-into-and-then-dipped-in-hot-water pin stripe. And both of them are in plain sight and mercifully not for sale.

Presumably the racks and rows of showcases full of hundreds of splendid suits ARE for sale but the salesman hasn't the least intention of showing them to you. Instead he regards his victim with an expression of impending nausea and says, "Now let's see, you take about a forty." He doesn't ask, he announces with sympathy and it is always the next size in the wrong direction for morale building, a size to make a fat man feel fatter, a short man feel shorter, and a skinny man run to his doctor for his annual check-up. The salesman then tacks back and

*"A teeny bit roomy, mmmm?"*

forth from the showcases on one side of the room to the other as though he has no idea which sizes are kept where. This proves to be true because his first few glances at the tags show that he was way off. I yearn to help him along by saying, "You're getting warmer, warmer, HOT," but I know that I am there only to keep George from escaping out the door prematurely, preferably not to be seen at all and certainly not to be heard. At last the salesman wedges apart a nearly impenetrable phalanx of suits and yanks out any old jacket which, "We'll just slip on for size." They could too, I mean both of them get into it because it is obviously a Jackie Gleason reject, all wool and two yards wide with sleeves as endless as a strait jacket's. From the trapped expression on George's face it probably is one in disguise.

"A teeny bit roomy, mmmm?" the sales-man hums in the understatement of the season and continues to riffle through the next hundred suits all of which look increasingly attractive but are obvi-ously out of bounds. The customer must not touch the merchandise because, of course, he doesn't know either his own size or his own preference. As a mat-ter of fact, at this point he doesn't know his own name, rank, and serial number.

Finally the salesman victoriously wrenches two suits out of the resistant racks and invariably one is purple and the other one is green.

"I was thinking of navy or Oxford gray," George murmurs as though apologizing for not being color blind, to which the salesman replies with one of three stock answers, "We're not showing those colors this season," or "They haven't come in yet, maybe in a month or so," or "Come, come, you don't want to wear an OLD suit!"

Oh he doesn't, eh? That's just what he does want to wear, if not the plus fours he had in college, then at least the wide-lapeled number in which he was married.

George continues to wear a retarded expression, the salesman goes through the motions of glancing at a few more labels, upside down, and then wringing his hands in mock despair, announces quite cheerfully, "Well, I'm afraid that's about it, in your size of course." Now oddly enough that was the very size we had in mind and to the salesman's evident surprise we can't seem to work up much enthusiasm for admiring his stock for giants or pigmies.

From a woman's point of view this is a discouraging moment, representing defeat on both sides. I frantically search for some cheerful remark to dispel the gloom only to realize that there is none to dispel. George's mood is positively euphoric. He straightens up, puts back on his authority and dignity with his old jacket, and surveys the establishment with approval if not downright fondness. In less than a minute he has undergone a personality change that could not be matched with an I.V. injection of diazepam. If fate had intended him to buy a suit he would have accepted the prognosis. But all tests were negative and he sails out of the store shriven, shoddy, and solvent for another six months.

## chapter 7

# How Come Doctors Never Go to the Doctor?

If there is any man who is cooperative with his colleagues professionally and uncooperative with them personally it is your friendly husband-M.D. The same chap who consults surgeons and radiologists when his patient has vertigo from hitting his head on the ice while retrieving the morning paper would rather spend the day with his own head between his knees than admit he was dizzy after he cracked his own cranium. He is far too busy, too knowledgeable, too chicken, and too distrustful to submit to the ministrations of another M.D.

My husband has never been hospitalized for illness and probably will not be unless he is unconscious. He has never even contemplated parting with his tonsils, appendix, or so much as a teeny, weeny wen. Until recently no one had listened to his heart or taken his blood pressure in twelve years and then only because it was required by the government for an overseas assignment. When I protested, "How do you know you don't have high blood pressure?" his thoughtful reply was, "Who wants to know?"

George doesn't intend to be stuck, probed, or have lights or instruments defile any of his orificia even if the instruments or lights are manipulated by his best-qualified peers. He is such a therapeutic nihilist that he gags on aspirin unless he is shaking so hard that his tremors are registering on the nearest seismograph. He is not unique in this. It is typical normal behavior for the followers of Hippocrates. During the second year in medical school every student is a hypochondriac. George had told me about one who saw his own vallate papillae and thought they were cancer. But after the second year, the only crocky doctors we have known have been bachelors and there aren't too many of those these days. Every doctor's wife in the country can give you an example of her man's ostrich-like behavior.

When George was an intern he yawned in front of the bathroom mirror one morning and saw a white coating on his tongue. His taste for cigarettes vanished with the premonition that he had leukoplakia, a precursor of carcinoma of the tongue. All day he dragged around convinced that his days were numbered, but of course he wouldn't admit this to another doctor. Finally he phoned a dentist friend and described his symptoms.

"Try to scrape it off," Kenneth said. "I'll hold on."

George was back in a minute. "It came off."

"Then forget it, but why are you mumbling?"

"Because I'm lighting a cigarette."

When George was a resident he came home with chills and fever and crawled into bed in his shorts without removing the bedspread. He lay there weighted down by three blankets and ten pounds of CECIL'S TEXTBOOK OF MEDICINE. By noon his self-diagnosis was meningitis. Towards evening he staggered into the bathroom and was startled to see that he was covered with light red maculopapules the size of pinheads.

"German measles!" he squawked happily, leaping into his trousers, "What's for supper?"

Does a mature internist change his spots? Last summer George picked up jungle rot, not in the South Pacific but from the floor of a locker room at a very fancy club. He shook a little athlete's foot powder on his feet and hoped the rot would go away if he ignored it. After a month and quite a lot of pressure from me he gingerly showed his desquamating extremity to a family physician whom he respects and trusts. But when, after an unsuccessful period of treatment with applications of another medication, his friend suggested a drug to be taken orally, he immediately looked the drug up in his PHYSICIANS' DESK REFERENCE, read the list of possible side effects, and flatly refused to take it. Months later, with both feet involved and little lumps called ids on his palms, bedeviled by itching and sloughing of scales like a sycamore tree, what was he doing about it? Nothing, of course.

George did perk up when he heard that the army sent its tinea patients to warm beaches where they could walk on the sand and bare their soles to the sun. But he wasn't convinced that the sun lamp and small box of sand that I offered as a substitute would have the same therapeutic effect. He thought that the long stretches of white sand, the palm trees, soft breezes, and salt water would be more benefi-

45

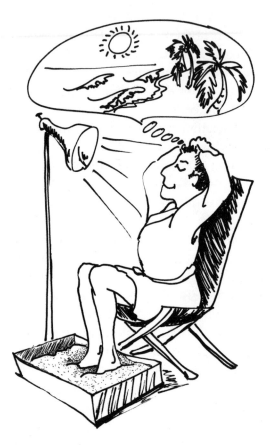

*"He thought that the long stretches of white sand, the palm trees, soft breezes, and salt water would be more beneficial."*

46

cial. They would be for almost anything, but he can't seem to find the long stretches of time.

You learn after a while that your M.D. husband won't use home remedies, won't discuss his problem with a whole medical school full of M.D.s, wouldn't dream of mentioning it to a dermatologist, and apparently hopes that the invading organisms will eventually become weaker from neglect and give up and so far they have, for all our medical friends seem to remain vertical most of the time. Of course they may feel awful but nothing short of traction will put an internist into the hands of a surgeon. It takes an aneurysm at least to get a surgeon to an internist and the family physician has always known that he sees the whole patient more clearly than do any of the specialists. Each of the other specialists believes that the family physician is competent in all fields except his, the specialist's, own specialty, but they all agree that the psychiatrists are crazier than any of them.

The medical care of physicians could be a specialty of its own, but who would be brave and foolish enough to devote his life to a group of patients who are recalcitrant, uncooperative, and usually invisible?

Will the physician heal himself? Certainly not, but nature probably will, and he will go on about his business of healing others even though the life he saves will never be his own.

# chapter  8

# Strangers in the
# Promised Land

The plight of the foreign wife in the United States was brought grimly to public attention several years ago when a young wife of a United Nations representative committed suicide. But after we all clucked in our monolingual tongues what did most of us do about it?

In an article appearing in an issue of RESIDENT PHYSICIAN a foreign doctor described some of the ways in which residents from other countries could help their wives adjust to American culture. This bootstrap effort is fine, but as hosts each year to thousands of young doctors and their wives from Iraq, Japan, Taiwan, and India shouldn't WE be doing something to give these young people a favorable impression of their residency in the United States?

At the University of Kansas Medical Center, an American resident's wife and the wife of an Iranian doctor who had lived in this country ten years decided to do something more than invite the foreign wives to an occasional tea at which they are largely ignored or looked at as curiosities rather than as people. In rounding up the wives of graduate students and residents from other countries they found that the loneliness was no myth. Most of these women are very well educated teachers, lawyers, technicians, or nurses, but many of them are not fluent in English. One girl stayed holed up in a tiny apartment day after day rather than face the embarrassment of her inability to communicate in English. One did all the laundry, including the baby's diapers, in the bathtub because she didn't know there was a Laundromat two blocks away, and, even if she had known about the Laundromat, who would show her how to use it? Many of these girls are used to large family households with brothers and sisters, uncles and aunts, and servants all milling around in noisy confusion. Perhaps this is why, in our country, most of them keep the radio or television on all day.

What they want is not a few crumbs from the tea table of the president's wife but a friend, an advocate, some American girls near their own age who are happy to have the opportunity of widening their own horizons while they are helping the foreign wives understand our language and culture.

At the University of Kansas Medical Center, a group called Mini-Mundo has been formed. Its members consist of American residents' wives and faculty wives as well as foreign wives. The program has evolved from need. English classes meet three times a week. A pre-school program has been set up so that young foreign children will be used to playing with English-speaking children before they enter American schools. Driving classes and help in interpreting our confusing traffic regulations have been popular. A cooking class with demonstrations and sampling of the foreigners' native dishes has been a favorite among the American wives. Group trips to museums, factories, historic sites, and restaurants have removed anxieties about getting around in the city. At Easter the older children colored eggs and hid them for the little children to find on the lawn of the Dean's house. No language barrier existed for the children. A tiny three-year-old South American girl clutched her basket firmly and dove into the bushes shouting "Huevos!" happily whenever she spotted another colored egg.

The Medical Center Auxiliary has sponsored the project to some extent with some of its members participating and with provision of some financial help for bus trips, refreshments, and materials. It is hoped that, through the auxiliary, American families will act as host families to newcomers from other countries, meeting them at the airports, guiding them through supermarkets, and showing them how to buy a man's shirt or a pair of pantyhose.

Helping is very simple, really. All you need to do is remember how you felt in a foreign country or even during your first day at college. You didn't need a formal organization. You needed a friend, someone to laugh with and to open a few doors that had looked like barricades until the handle was turned for you and the door opened to a new world in which you were no longer lonely because you had a friend.

# chapter 9

# Keep Moving, Please

Why let your next moving day be relaxed and casual when, with a little effort, you can turn it into a real mess?

Any dedicated wife and mother can create a truly moving experience for the whole family by following the time-tested tips listed below.

• Plan ahead. Notify the phone company to disconnect the phone well in advance. This guarantees that you will have no phone to use on the day of the move. Movers encourage this because it prevents you from calling their office at eight-thirty, nine, and nine-fifteen to ask where the boys are.

• Start early. Set the alarm and just before dawn leap out of bed and pull the sheets out from under your husband. It puts him in a gala mood for the whole day. His bellowing will also wake the children who can then get a head start in getting in the way.

• Heckle the family through breakfast so that you can get the dishes into the dishwasher, and close it. If you don't have a dishwasher, hide the dishes in the sink. You'll never miss them until you start counting plates and juice glasses at the new address.

*"Why let your next moving day be relaxed and casual when, with a little effort, you can turn it into a real mess?"*

• Remove your name and number from the mailbox so that the movers can spend another half hour, at your expense, touring the neighborhood.

• When the van lumbers into sight and you realize that the awful moment is at hand, ease your tension by rushing out and shouting at the driver so that he will back over your neighbor's lawn. The wheel tracks make interesting drainage ditches and if a few treasured white birches crumple beneath the cab the driver and your neighbor's wife can discuss the lawsuit (at your expense) giving you an extra ten minutes to apply eyeliner and empty the ice trays.

• Pack all important papers and the keys to the house you're leaving and the one you're moving into in a small bag and place the bag near the door so that the movers can load it into the van first. This insures that it will be the last article unpacked at your destination and that all your shabby furniture, spread out on the lawn, can be assessed by your new neighbors at one time.

• As soon as you arrive at the new house send the children to play in the neighbor's yard so that they won't be under the movers' feet. This guarantees that you'll meet your new neighbors almost at once in a very informal manner.

• Tell the movers that the front door of the new house is two inches wider than it actually is. In that way they can wedge the refrigerator onto the front steps and block the door before they discover that both the front door and the door of the refrigerator will have to be removed.

• Pack an extra screwdriver, a pen, checkbook, and toilet paper in a secret place so that when you need them no one can remember where they are.

• Stand at the door and give the movers exact instructions as to where each piece of furniture is to be placed. For example, don't say, "That goes in the first bedroom on the left." Say, "In Patty's room." If they wonder aloud who Patty is, call her in and introduce her. It's always nice to keep things on a social basis.

• If you are not moving a long distance, rent a truck and move all the small articles yourself. It will only take ten round trips and can be done in a day and a half, maybe.

• Pack books in big cartons because these will hold many books. Your husband may not be able to get the cartons off the ground without dislocating his back, but if you are making the move at the most sensible time, which is during his vacation, he can spend the next ten days flat on his back without missing a day of work. Rent an open truck so that when it starts to pour in transit all the cartons will begin to soften and fall apart. This will make the books a little slippery but much more accessible.

• Save packing fees by carrying sharp tools and the contents of the bathroom cabinets loose in a waste basket. Then, when you empty your basket and cut your finger on a loose razor blade, the bandages will be handy.

• Tell the former owners of your new house not to bother to take their discarded junk to the dump. After all, as soon as you have unpacked you will have to go to the dump anyway. In the meantime your children can have fun poking through and scattering a whole new collection of bent coat hangers, Hawaiian leis, and frayed sneakers. This compensates for your cruelty in prying their little hands loose from an almost identical junk pile that you left behind.

• When the movers have finally folded

their quilts like the Arabs and not so silently stolen away, don't let the ensuing peace depress the family. Plan little surprises. Tell the children that the next day they are going to have booster shots. Regale your husband with the news that your mother is coming for a nice long visit. If you spring all these exciting plans simultaneously, everyone will start crying at once and you can drown out their wails while you're trying out the new shower, comforted by the knowledge that through your efforts the whole family has been moved to tears.

# chapter 10

# Doctor, Your Face Needs Lifting

"I wish my doctor was more like Marcus Welby."

I heard it first at the airport, which, as a matter of fact, is one of the best places to hear the grass roots growing. The only trouble is that most of the time you can't hear anything because of interference from jets and announcers. By the time the tumult and the shouting had died my wistful gentleman had gone about his business.

But it was only a few days later that I heard a variation on the same theme.

"Dr. Welby is more real than my real doctor."

This time I was able to capture the owner of the voice crying in the medical wilderness and ask her what she meant by real.

"Well, he seems to care about his patients. I don't want tests. I want tender loving care."

Don't we all? But as a doctor's wife I have been brainwashed into leaning on tests and have long since adjusted to the hard fact that t.l.c., of which there is a limited supply, is apt to be reserved for OTHER people, the ones not related to a doctor. Also, being a doctor's wife, I had, of course, never watched "Marcus Welby, M.D." And if you found a doctor watching a medical program you'd take a colleague aside and suggest a psychiatric consultation.

But maybe the time has come when you should watch it. "Marcus Welby, M.D." is telling you something, doctor, and if you don't listen you'll soon be hearing it from your patients. Or you won't be hearing from your patients at all because they will have bundled up their symptoms and carried them away to an M.D. who can read the handwriting on the T.V. screen.

There is at least one who has deciphered it, the handwriting on the T.V. screen, that is. Dr. Michael Halberstam, an internist in Washington, D.C., wrote a lead article for the NEW YORK TIMES MAGAZINE. Brushed aside in favor of a make-believe doctor, hurt, and being a true scientist, he decided to do a complete work-up on the T.V. series and come up with a diagnosis. He wrote, "After a total immersion course in Welby, I am convinced I've met my match." This is because Dr. Welby, unlike other television doctors, is not a specialist who discovers an unknown disease in the laboratory or a surgeon who performs a miracle in the operating room of a large city hospital. He is a general practitioner for whom the Doe family has more nostalgia than for the general store or a five-cent subway ride. He is not sexy and surly like Ben Casey, as introspective as Dr. Kildare, or snarly like old Dr. Gillespie. To

60

Dr. Halberstam's surprise, he found the show to be authentic and technically almost perfect, for which the credit goes to The American Academy of Family Physicians who hover over it, well, like a family physician!

The secret of the series' success and Dr. Welby's appeal is something that is not new in medicine but may have become temporarily mislaid until the increasingly vocal public and the new crop of medical students began muttering about it some time ago. It focuses on the patient, not the illness. The occupant of Room 421 is not a peptic ulcer. It is Tom Elwood who has just lost two large advertising accounts, whose son has just dropped out of college, and whose daughter shares her bed and board with a young revolutionary who is allergic to razors and regular employment. It is the patient who has to live with the disease, who is in trouble, not the crater in his stomach.

I can already hear you protesting that you are aware of the whole patient and that you could give not only more intensive but more comprehensive medical care if you, like Dr. Welby, had only one patient to worry about at a time. But, unfortunately, each patient wants you to be as concerned with his or her problems as though he or she WERE your only patient. He or she doesn't really want you to have outside interests such as a wife, children, or a golf game. It's no accident that neither Dr. Welby or his handsome young assistant, Dr. Kiley, are married. That's just the way the viewer ordered his fantasy. Oddly enough the ladies warm up more to Dr. Welby than to the younger doctor. They are not looking for vicarious romance. They can find that on the movie re-runs any night in the week. They are looking for "someone to watch over me."

Perhaps it will coat your own ulcer to learn, Doctor, that this program has done a good deal to polish up the tarnished image of physicians because patients want a doctor who is believable. They want to respect and admire him. In spite of what some of the medical students are currently advocating, the average patient doesn't want his doctor to be just one of the boys. He wants to respect his doctor's academic training and experience, to be comforted by his compassion and wisdom, and to receive dedicated attention above and beyond the call of duty. What brought patients to Hippocrates' marble bench or your waiting room has not changed in over two thousand years. Spoken or unspoken, the words in the patient's mind are, "I'm sick. I'm scared. I need your help."

*chapter 11*

# "O Wad Some Power the Giftie Gie Us to See Oursels as Others See Us!"

You might as well face it. You have a split personality. Not just plain split, it's fractured.

Before you rush off to look up schizophrenia let me reassure you. You're not that kind of a nut. You're another kind, a doctor's wife.

But fortunately your chameleon characteristics are only in the eyes of the beholder. You know that you are loyal, trustworthy, and all the other girl-scout adjectives, but your image in the eyes of your children, your husband and his nurses and patients is as distorted as your reflection in those mirrors in the funny house at an amusement park.

In the eyes of your children you are only a part-time mother, being constantly pulled away from them by their father's phone calls and his changed plans, and by having to take over more of their father's chores than do other mothers in the neighborhood.

In the eyes of your husband you cater exclusively to the whims of the children, the call of the P.T.A., the church, and the Ladies Auxiliary (which he calls the axilla). After all, if he had wanted to marry Indira Gandhi or the mother of the year he would have. No shadow of a doubt clouds his eyes in contemplation of the delight of any one of these ladies at being chosen for the honor of being his wife. He may even quote part of the marriage ceremony, "And forsaking all others, cleave only unto him." You may have interpreted that to mean that you were to bid adieu to former boy friends and not go looking for any new ones in the future either. But he includes children, churches, college classmates, and clubs in an evil force hell-bent on separating your attention from where it would be well spent, on him.

Now step to the next mirror, please, and see yourself as your husband's office nurse, the head nurse in the O.R., or any nurse who sees you. Oh, the poor doctors! Why they let themselves be trapped by undedicated, demanding, prolific women who know so little about a doctor's life! With all the capable, loyal, trustworthy, attractive, and well-trained women who are nurses and therefore qualified to be doctors' wives it is such a waste to see doctors tied down to just ordinary women, i.e., not nurses. I've never heard this said, mind you, because I am not a nurse, but if it isn't true I'll eat the next starched white cap, lavender ribbon, ruffles and all that I see.

A secretary sees you as through a glass darkly, but whether the glass is rose-colored or streaked is pretty much up to you. It is easy enough to keep not only the peace, but even a form of mutual admiration if you give each other enough room to put up a circus tent. I never wanted George's secretary to pull Debbie's thumb out of her mouth, comment on the length of my skirt, or rearrange the casseroles in my kitchen cabinet, so what right have I to muck around in her domain? Of course I don't want her thumb in George's mouth or him eating her casseroles either, but that's neither here nor there at the moment, and I'm awfully glad it's not here. When a doctor is opening an office he'll probably need his wife's help in decorating the office, but that's before the advent of his secretary. George's secretaries have always been very capable. They could keep more than two things in mind at once without fusing them. Their hands flew over the typewriter keys like butterflies and they have had the knack of looking band-box fresh, as though they'd been immobilized in amber, which I can admire better than I can emulate.

And now the last mirror, the one that shows how you look in the patient's eyes. I don't seem to see any image in that mirror at all. There isn't any. In the patient's eyes the doctor's wife doesn't exist. The patient wants to feel that he has the doctor's full attention. He needs to believe that the doctor is just a bit superhuman. It is distasteful to think of him zipping up the back of your dress, brushing his teeth, or tripping over the cat on the cellar steps.

If you can help it you should never show your face to the patients. It may be the face that launched a thousand ships but the patients regard it as a destroyer.

I'll never forget the look on a patient's face

when George was first in practice. We still lived in Cockroach Hall. George had just outfitted his new office on Madison Avenue. He had seen this patient, a Philippine diplomat's wife, in his office, but for some reason the patient and her husband came to the apartment unexpectedly. The door was open into the hall as usual to allow the comings and, hopefully, the goings of all the children in the building. George was in his shirt-sleeves and I was lying on the couch with my shoes off. There was a knock on the door. At our shouted, "Come in," in tripped a tiny immaculate chauffeur followed by a tiny immaculate man in a black chesterfield and a homburg, and a tiny immaculate woman wrapped in mink. The eyes of the three darted in horror from George's shirt-sleeves to my large western feet, and then dropped to the floor in disillusionment.

Another patient, who firmly believes that George saved his life, subsequently became a friend, and though George has not been in practice for years, he still pictures George with a halo and me as not really existent. He is very polite to me and to the girls, but his eyes follow George around the room like a collie dog's.

Our culture isn't far enough removed from the witch doctors and the medicine men to be able to mix social life and professional life without destroying the magic.

But even though you feel as if you were in front of a three-way mirror, with each glass shaped to distort in another dimension, the image your husband cares about bears a strong resemblance to that snapshot he carries in his wallet. It may take a little longer to look like the snapshot when you are elbow deep in cookie dough and your hair looks as though you had combed it with the eggbeater, but after looking at edematous ankles, sclerotic eyegrounds, and luetic rashes all day, your husband longs for the sight of a healthy, smiling face, and the pedestal on which he prefers to see it displayed is your neck.

Can she bake a cherry pie, smile like Jackie Onassis, and bring home a pay check every Friday night? All positive findings. But the $R_x$ for a doctor's wife includes another ingredient not listed in the U.S. Pharmacopeia. This ingredient is still something of a mystery to me in spite of the years I've spent as the wife of a medical student, intern, resident, internist, professor, and dean—all the same chap.

I've known a lot of spouses with spice. Some also had humility, humor, and an auxiliary supply of what used to be called charm. Put them all together and they spell something. Maybe it is character.

When I was growing up, children's brains were washed regularly in the theory that frustrating experiences built character. I was denied the second-degree badge at camp because of table manners, after nearly killing myself perfecting the crawl and learning to identify thirty types of ferns. Flunking out on this award was supposed to firm up my backbone and put stars in my eyes. But the stars were rained out by my tears and my only firm purpose was to find a corner in which to lick my wounds. Maybe the incident led to an improvement in my table manners, but I'm sure it had precious little to do with character building.

The effort continued, however, and by the time I was in high school, meagerly equipped for the

Junior Prom with a long and shapeless figure, equally long and shapeless dress, and glasses that came to rest halfway down my long and shapeless nose, I was supposed to welcome being stuck with one boy. However, this boy's feet and mine tangled like soccer players scuffling for the ball, while the boys in the stag line, whom I had known since first grade, stared fixedly over my head with a total lack of recognition.

Somehow character didn't seem to be what the boys were looking for. I would have swapped the best character reference for a beat-up corsage any old Saturday night.

But finally a college degree, a doctor husband, and two children, none of which was awarded on the basis of moral fiber, made me recklessly suppose that I was no longer prey to those agonizing experiences calculated to spur me onward and upward to character development.

So it was with a gay heart that I welcomed the news that George was being considered for the deanship of the Medical College at the University of Vermont. Five years before we had bought a little hillside farm with a brook, waterfall, and natural swimming pool in Jericho, Vermont, only seventeen miles from the campus in Burlington. Every summer we overloaded the car and fled to the country in May, where the children and I stayed from the first bluet to the last aster. We were getting fed up with New York and we loved Vermont with the fierce possessiveness of city dwellers who have recently put down a slender root in the country. George's prospective new job in the part of the country we loved was meant for us, we were sure, and it only remained to convince the appointment committee that George was meant for them.

There was no need for me to go to Burlington with George for the interview. The excuse that I could go on to the farm and cut down a Christmas tree from our own woods served as well as any for me tagging along to Vermont. We parked the children with their grandparents and headed north with high hopes.

The next morning George set off for a day of interviews and appointments and I stuffed myself into a Morgan Memorial assortment of stadium boots, storm coat, mittens, and wool cap and took off for the hinterland.

Several inches of snow cushioned the meadows and left a marshmallow on each fencepost. Mt. Mansfield and Camel's Hump were marble white on top but the lesser mountains had a prickly crewcut look and were purpled with long shadows. The driveway to our little house had disappeared under the snow so I left the car at the side of the road, and, armed with saw and hatchet, floundered up through the rocky pasture to the woods.

Each potential Christmas tree turned out to be flat in back where it was squashed up against another tree. The few well-shaped ones were either too small to satisfy the children or too unwieldy to satisfy me. I finally talked myself into a choice and flailed away with the hatchet before I could change my mind again. Somehow the hatchet never struck twice in the same spot. I nicked and gouged until the small trunk looked like an I.B.M. card. At last, down on all fours, with the scratchy lower branches raking my face and unloading their burden of snow down my neck, I sawed the scarred and battered trunk through. The tree stood a moment, then quivered and toppled with a sigh, fragrant with fresh resin. I grasped the sticky, prickly butt in one mittened hand, the hatchet and saw in the other, and staggered down the hill to the car.

The day was beautiful. The Christmas tree, if cockeyed, was our own. The blue and purple countryside looked like the Swiss Christmas cards I al-

"*. . . but when I withdrew my hand the mitten stayed in his.*"

ways admired in the Madison Avenue bookstores, and a great new adventure lay ahead.

Face scratched, streaked with pitch, blue lips weirdly rimmed with that morning's lipstick, wool hunting cap askew, I charged up the hotel steps and pushed through the door, elated by my personal triumph as a woodsman. My glasses immediately steamed up, blinding me totally, but a familiar voice was coming through the fog.

"Maggie," George was saying, "This is Dr. McKay, Dr. Amidon, and Dr. Pierce. They are the committee from the medical college and they thought they'd like to see what my wife is like."

They could see all right! I was the only blind one. They could see my runny nose, ridiculous outfit, and idiotic grin. I reached out one soggy mitten and shook Dr. McKay's hand, but when I withdrew my hand the mitten stayed in his. A mixture of pitch and wet wool covered his palm when he finally ripped free.

"How nice!" I croaked. "If you think I look battle-scarred, you should see the tree."

I backed into the elevator hoping that it would whisk me into oblivion, but, as the operator waited for George to join me, I thought I heard one of the doctors say, "That's all we needed now, a real character!"

That was the end. Maybe I deserved it, but as the elevator rose my heart stayed down with my stomach. I had gummed everything up.

"What did he say?" I groaned to George, dreading the reply. But George's face was beaming. "He said," George answered happily, "that's all we needed to know. REAL CHARACTER!"

*chapter* *12*

# Shoemakers' Children

Feast or famine is the medical fare served up to the doctor's family. Although I've had my moments of doubt, I prefer the back of the doctor's hand to a palm full of prescriptions, pills, and proctoscopes. Our children have not always agreed. Our older daughter stamped into the house in a rage, when she was in first grade, shouting, "Why can't I be constipated like the other kids?" When she was required to have a physical exam for college it was her initial encounter with the mysteries of gowns, blood tests, and urinalysis.

Our medicine cabinet isn't empty. It contains the same assortment of non-medical articles as it did before we had children plus phalanxes of shampoos, hair sprays, tubes of eye shadow, and moisturizing foundation. There are brushes of every size for eyelashes, eye lining, and even for teeth and hair. But there still aren't any medicines. Well, hardly any. In the course of the years I have managed to smuggle in one bottle of aspirin and a tired sample of powder for treatment of athlete's foot, but these items cower behind their well-touted shelf mates.

There is a doctor in the house but his

chronic condition of therapeutic nihilism makes him allergic to antibiotics, vitamin pills, and allergies. For years his family's bones have swung with the slaloms. Not one of us has had a fractured anything unless you count the toe George broke showing off for his new son-in-law. And, of course, that toe was never set. George just limped around in a pair of loose moccasins for six weeks until it gave up and stopped hurting. Our children learned at their father's knee that there is only one of two possible answers to the question, "What should I do about this, Daddy?" Either "Soak it" or "Forget it."

I know there are many doctors' families who have built-in continuous medical anxiety. They can have it. One friend of ours does throat cultures of his children every time they open their mouths. I don't dare look closely at the cross-stitched sampler in their bedroom because I am afraid it might read, "Home is where the Q-T waves."

Another colleague tattoos his offspring with flu shots, cold shots, $B_{12}$, and some distillate of maple syrup because he says they are allergic to the pollen from maple trees in the spring. Another ailing outfit has been x-rayed so often that even I could guess at the diagnosis, radiation poisoning.

The exception that proves our household rule took place at the time that Debbie came home from school with all the symptoms of cystitis. In this instance George's ears snapped to attention, which is enough to frighten any doctor's child. Debbie was whisked to see the top renal researcher, who ran her through a series of tests. Her symptoms disappeared in twelve hours. The reactions to the tests were negative. The urologist was undaunted and, with George's

74

approval, had the tests repeated; Debbie had to go back and be followed for a year. Reactions to all tests remained negative. Everyone was puzzled. Everyone but Debbie.

"I keep telling you I used that new bubble bath," she protested.

Sometime later a nurse in the renal clinic of a pediatric hospital told me she had observed the same phenomenon in several young female patients who had lolled in that same sudsy heaven. It was not the sort of controlled experiment that gets written up in the JOURNAL but it won Debbie over to the "soak it" or "forget it" school of thought.

Of course we've carried the casual attitude too far on several occasions. Murmurs of nausea from the young while on an automobile trip should be heeded instantly. There is hardly time between the first "I don't feel good" and the first retch to pull to the side of the road and eject the small green patient and her head-holding mama. In every doctor's home there are also borderline cases in which it is very difficult to distinguish between early morning aches and pains that indicate the onset of illness and similar symptoms that indicate reluctance to go to school. A cross teacher, an unfinished assignment, or a pet snake in a boy's pocket can produce headache, anorexia, and even vomiting between seven and eight in the morning. I defy any doctor's wife to be infallible in the differentiation between the onset of flu and the onset of stage fright.

I packed Patty off to the Brearley School in New York one morning only to have her returned promptly by an indignant teacher with a note from the school physician. By the time my little homing

75

pigeon had completed the round trip her temperature registered 103 degrees. She was sick all right. No one would then or now call that pediatrician an alarmist. He is one of the most relaxed and reassuring M.D.s in the country and by now he has royalties to prove it. His name is Benjamin Spock.

In defense of the doctor in the family I must say that while knowing the patient helps in diagnosis, being related by paternity makes the doctor look at his child with blurred, double, or too sharply focused vision. He has to hold his child off at arm's length to see him clearly. He is not unaware of his family's health; he just prefers to assume it to be good. And when you finally get through to him by trailing around dragging bloody bandages or holing up in bed at noon, he looks so woebegone that you are consumed with guilt and prop yourself up, stuff yourself into your clothes, and insist that you could lick your weight in wildcats.

He may not always know what you or the children have, but he knows what you haven't and that is very reassuring. When he says your stiff neck is not meningitis, the neck hurts just the same but your anxiety is cured.

This reminds me of a remark made by a worried patient when George told her she did not have cancer.

"Oh, I'm so glad, Doctor," she said. "Now I know that when I die it won't be from something serious!"

When I had a violent earache following a plane trip and was in such obvious distress that George threw precedent to the winds and took me to an ENT man, the specialist's comment to George

*"'Oh, I'm so glad, Doctor,' she said. 'Now I know that when I die it won't be from something serious!'"*

went something like this: "I don't know why that drum didn't rupture. Look at that color! That's a classic. I'd certainly like the students to see that ear." I was ignored. These doctors obviously weren't worried so why should I be? I began to be rather proud of my bulging eardrum. What did they do about it? Why nothing, of course. The ache went away after a month. The ear doesn't even crackle, pop, or gurgle anymore.

If it is medical treatment for the family that you want, you should have counted a few more buttons and stopped on lawyer or merchant. These men buy medical care the way we buy groceries or shoes for the children. Can you imagine living like that? Of course not, and better not try because it's not in your future. That's for OTHER people. You are different. You are a doctor's wife.

## chapter  13

# The New
# Doctor's Wife,
# She Ain't What
# She Used to Be!

Now wait a minute. What did she used to be?

That depends partly on where she used to be. If she was a city doctor's wife fifty years ago she was even less likely to darken his office door and hold the patient's hand than most city doctors' wives are today. The farther away from the city the doctor settled, the more active his wife was in the care of his patients. The counterpart of Norman Rockwell's picture of the country doctor sitting by the patient's bedside was the doctor's wife, swaddled in a flannel wrapper, heating up coffee in a blue enameled pot on the back of the wood-burning range, waiting for the sound of the wheels of the doctor's buggy in the dooryard. Those were the days when tonsils were sometimes removed from the patient while he lay on the kitchen table, when babies were delivered at home, and neighbors, relatives, or the doctor's wife sat up all night with the patient.

What the doctor's wife used to be was a pair of hands and emotional support. Now she is a mind. She is not sitting on her hands nor has she given up her supportive role, but she rarely practices the nursing skills, because even the nursing skills are not what they used to be. This is the effect of technology on participation in the modern health-care system. Medical care has become much more dependent on laboratory work, diagnostic procedures, and radiology. Blood samples obtained from patients in northern Vermont are flown to California for the laboratory work because this is less expensive than maintaining laboratories nearby. If the doctor's wife were a combination medical technologist, an intensive-care nurse, an x-ray technician, and a computer expert she would be a super robot but hardly the young doctor's dream of someone nice to come home to.

Does this mean that she has been programmed out of her role as a doctor's wife? I made an informal survey among a few elderly doctors' wives, a few brand-new doctors' wives, and the vast majority who are all too aware that they are no longer young but certainly do not want to be considered old, ranging in years from thirty to sixty. Surprisingly enough all three groups came up with very similar answers. They all agreed that the doctor's wife of fifty years ago, twenty-five years ago, and now was and is service oriented. It is the type of service that has changed. Whereas she used to be active at her husband's elbow or, if she was a town or city wife, hospital oriented in terms of auxiliary work, she now is community oriented. She is involved with the League of Women Voters; child welfare; tutoring programs for high school drop-outs; mental health; ecology; Meals on Wheels; Planned Parenthood; senior-citizen recreation programs; Health Career Days; drug-abuse education; reclamation centers for bottles, cans, and newspapers; and/or the prevention of the extinction of the bald eagle. How many of these enterprises were a part of her grandmother's day? Such involvement is in addition to the care and feeding of her husband and children or arranging for the care and feeding of them. And I'll risk showing my age and inclinations by saying that for her husband's and children's sakes I hope that she is stirring the pots and drying the tears. If mental health and nutrition are important enough for her to campaign about they are even more important for her to attend to at home.

The doctor's wife may not be what she used to be but she just might be someone quite a bit more effective. Let's not spend too much time mourning the good old days in patient care. The laying on of hands was very reassuring for the patient's family but in many cases it was all the doctor had to offer. It didn't cure the patient of mastoiditis, diptheria, or typhoid fever. It was palliative rather than preventive.

The doctor's wife has come out of the old-fashioned kitchen where she used to hold an ether cone over the patient's face and she is now trying to clean up the air we all must breathe in order to live. Her environment has broadened to include the world. The world is her oyster and she is trying to make sure that that oyster won't give you hepatitis!

# chapter 14

# The Care and Feeding of House Guests

During the nine years when George was dean of the Medical College at the University of Vermont, during the school year we lived on a ninety-acre farm three miles outside of Burlington. The big cowbarn was filled with bags of superphosphate in various stages of disintegration, bales of hay, the twitterings of barn swallows, and the cooing of pigeons who lived under the eaves. Upstairs the horse barn was filled with loose hay and downstairs with a temperamental riding horse, two dedicated pigs, several dull-eyed sheep, and, after school hours, any number of bright-eyed children. At night, any number of green-eyed cats held sway. The chicken house bulged with one hundred and twenty-five chickens. It also played host to more rats than I care to admit, but these creatures were not invited. In fact, my intolerance of them and their intolerance of D-Con kept their census pretty low.

The attic of the house sheltered our beloved ghosts of the Fay family who had built our house one hundred and fifty years earlier. The second floor was occupied by four Wolfs, and the first floor now and then harbored an itinerant population of house guests. The cellar was unoccupied except from May first to June fifteenth when twelve exceptionally stupid turkey poults added their peculiar noises and distinctive aroma to the whole atmosphere of the dwelling.

It soon became apparent that my new role as a dean's wife was not so much pouring tea as conveying food. I fed one hundred and fifty mouths, beaks, snouts, and muzzles every day or else I heard a lot of cackles, whinnies, baas, grunts, meows, and "when do we eat?"'s about it. Fresh from many years in Manhattan, I loved every minute. Well, almost every minute. Life with animals, children, a husband, and visiting firemen is bound to produce one predictable crisis every twenty-four hours and unpredictable ones when guests are in residence, which meant that college presidents, deans, pathologists, and neurologists were occasionally pressed into service above and beyond the educational purpose they had come to serve.

We lived only a stone's throw, if you had a good throwing arm, from the airport. This made me official greeter. I could wait till I heard the plane overhead before I dried my hands on the dish towel and took off in the red truck for the airport. To the credit of our guests, I can't remember one who blanched at the sight of a red Ford pick-up instead of a limousine. The visitors heaved their suitcases or attaché cases in with the grain bags or lumber, swung up into the cab, and on their first trip uniformly pronounced, "This is the life!"

That was before they were pressed into service.

I picked up Hugh Luckey one day because George was in a meeting. At that time, Hugh was dean at Cornell and I doubt if he had had much previous experience with baby chicks. But the chicks were waiting at the post office, two big vibrating, peeping cartons of them, and Hugh gallantly put them into the back of the truck. Our next stop was the loading platform of the Pease Grain Company to annex a hundred pounds of chick mash and fifty of small grit. It was a warm day, which the chicks and I welcomed, but by the time we got home, set up the brooder, transplanted one hundred downy, yellow peepers into their new quarters in the chicken house, and emptied the bags into the feed bin, Hugh's dark suit was powdered with calcium dust and mash, his face was red and glistening, and he was happy to get out of his wet shirt and into a dry martini. But he had entered into the spirit of rural life and was so entranced with five tiny, month-old kittens, who were pouncing over and under the couch, his legs, and the martini glass, that he happily accepted our offer of twin kittens to take home to his twin sons. It was at the time of a milk strike in New York and, having four temporarily milk-starved children at home in Bronxville, he was delighted that Vermont was flowing with milk and maple syrup. So he boarded his plane with a gallon of maple syrup, eight quarts of milk, and two kittens whose pansy faces peered out of his brief case. I'll never forget the stewardess' expression. She looked at the kittens and then at the eight quarts of milk and with a straight face asked, "Are you sure that will be enough to last them all the two hours to New York?"

Dr. John Kidd arrived one day for a pathology meeting. He was a very dignified and formal professor. I was grateful that George had left me the "soft car" as a taxi, and secretly hoped that the children would be more civil and silent than was their wont when Mama waved the red flag of apprehension. Dinner was achieved without catastrophe. The children went to bed and George and Dr. Kidd were talking quietly in the living room when Patty's small voice came down the stairs.

"Mommy, I can't go to sleep. My doll carriage is making funny noises. I think Mitty's in it."

Mitty was our beloved and prolific mother cat. She was in the doll carriage in Patty's room all right but she wasn't alone. There were four slick, wet, newborn kittens moiling around groping for sustenance.

Dr. Kidd's formality evaporated. He leaped up the stairs, solicitously helped George carry the doll carriage and its occupants down into the playroom and hung over the carriage purring louder than Mitty. The cat had loosened his tongue. He laughed and chatted about his family and was as relaxed as an old shoe.

The next morning when I was stumbling around the kitchen assembling breakfast, I thought I heard someone talking in the playroom. There was Dr. Kidd, grinning sheepishly and holding a lap-full of kittens.

"Just making early morning rounds," he shouted gaily. "I thought they might be lonesome."

We always anticipated a visit from Dr. Harold Wolff with a mixture of delight and nervousness. He had been George's professor of neurology at Cornell and he and George had worked together on various research projects. George's admiration for him bordered on idolatry but there was nothing chummy about their friendship. Dr. Wolff did everything on a precise, split-second schedule. He was compulsive, demanding, probing, impatient, and exciting. He could make you feel exalted or two-headed and often both. He also looked as though he had been dressed by a valet and then lacquered.

The visit that I remember best, because it was unfortunately the last before his death, was scheduled down to the last moment. He had appointments all day, was to go on a tour with George, and then come back to our house for a cocktail party with a group of doctors who had been invited to meet him. I had checked out the guest room à la a marine sergeant, scoured the bathroom, put out fresh towels and washcloth. The canapes were ready and the guests due to arrive at any minute.

Dr. Wolff and George rushed in and Dr. Wolff hustled into the bathroom to take a quick shower. In my excitement I hadn't heard that the pump had been chugging away for some time. If I had, I would have dashed upstairs and seen that the upstairs toilet had been left running. Our water supply emanated from a well that had been dug in the meadow. There was plenty of water in the well but the long pipe leading from it was of small diameter and if too much water was used at one time or for too long a time, the pump couldn't keep up with the demand, and so it sucked hoarsely at the bottom of the tank stirring up dark, rusty sludge.

Too late I heard the gasps of the pump! I hurtled down the cellar stairs. The pressure was down to five. I dashed up to the second floor and reseated the offending rubber thing in the back of the toilet. But I knew all too well that, instead of a spray of clear hot water, Dr. Wolff was being deluged by spurts of copper-colored gunk. I hovered near his door apprehensively and soon he appeared, band-box fresh as ever, smiling and relaxed.

"I'm so sorry—the shower—the pump—the mud," I stammered.

"Oh, THAT!" he waved his hand airily, grinning. "I thought it was just part of your rugged rural regimen."

When Dr. Wolff was surrounded by the guests I sneaked into his bathroom. No sign of any mud. Everything had been wiped clean; the towel neatly folded. I unfolded the towel. To my horror it was not only streaked with mud and rust, there was a huge bite out of the middle of it. During a visit with us, my thrifty mother had neatly hemmed all around a plate-sized hole in the center of the towel. Folded in the linen closet it had looked faultless to me. Our distinguished visitor had not only been pelted with mud but also had had to dry himself with a terry-cloth doughnut!

*chapter* 15

# The Dilemma of the Black Doctor's Wife

If you think your image as a doctor's wife is fractured by the pull of family demands, community expectations, and your own interests, color yourself black and you'll know how it really feels to be a jigsaw puzzle.

All doctors' wives have certain problems in common. They have too little of their husbands' time and help with family matters, too much of a goldfish-bowl existence, bizarre medical care, and a special fatigue from sitting on pedestals that don't fit. But the problems of the black doctor's wife are doubled by the fact that she is black.

What do I know about it? Very little until recently. Like the average well-intentioned but poorly informed white woman, I have a lot of waking up to do. But, with the help of friends who are black doctors' wives, I am becoming aware of the special problems of the black doctor and his wife.

Although, as doctors' wives and members of the same county auxiliary, white and black doctors' wives have a common base, the black doctors' wives agree that their problems are caused more by race than by profession. Their present difficulties are those of all educated black people today. They have to try harder than most white people do to get the best education available, and to improve their environment, their living conditions, and their children's opportunities, only to be met now with criticism from the ghetto and militant black people as well as the large ostrich population among the white community.

Their goals used to be to attain the white middle-class standards in education, housing, and environment. But now middle-class values have been declared false by many young people, white as well as black, and by activists of all ages. If the black doctor does not work and live in the ghetto he is accused of not having a social conscience; if he does he is often considered inferior to his counterpart in the suburbs.

Few of us, if we are honest, would choose to live in the ghetto and even if we voluntarily put up with the discomforts of poverty—the dirt, the crowded conditions, the high prices for low-quality products—we are reluctant to inflict inferior education, dubious companionship, and physical and emotional danger on our children. Everyone wants adequate medical attention, adequate schools, and adequate housing. Everyone should have them, but they rarely are available in the ghetto.

To start with the education of the black doctor, we are all aware that the exceptionally bright, well-qualified black applicant to medical colleges is being wooed by the predominately white medical schools which are being pressured within and without to increase the enrollment of black students. Those few are sought after as students and now as interns and residents. But what about their opportunities when they are ready to practice? They must often practice where they may, not where they choose. Their housing will be limited and the education of their children may have to be separate and unequal. By this I mean they may have to send their children to private schools in order to insure them equal educational opportunities.

Advances have been made and are being made, but unfortunately some of them are quite recent and the result of violent demonstrations which we all deplore.

One black doctor's wife told me that in one community an exception was made to allow her children to go to the "better" public school because her husband was a doctor. But what about the other black children?

In one Midwestern town, one black doctor and his family were welcomed. They were the only black family in a small town where the doctor was needed and wanted. All was friendly socially until the children reached the age at which there were boy–girl parties. Then suddenly the children were no longer included in any social activities. They had to accept isolation or move to a larger city.

A black doctor's wife who was an Episcopalian went to the Episcopal church in the town where they had just moved and was turned away. She couldn't become instant white, so she became instant Baptist.

The discrimination is not all white–black. At a civic meeting a black doctor's wife was introduced to a young black activist who immediately said, "You know the people in the ghetto don't care that you are a doctor's wife. That means nothing to them." She wasn't the one who told him she was a doctor's wife nor had she any intention of standing on her husband's shoulders. In fact, when her own little boy was not invited into the other children's homes in the neighborhood into which her family had moved, she made a point to take the neighborhood children everywhere she took her children. After a while one neighbor, who was also black, warmed up and said, "You know, you are really very nice for a doctor's wife."

Other black doctors' wives face criticism from their relatives. They become accustomed to, but don't enjoy, the constant refrain of, "If I had your opportunities I would be somebody too."

The critics usually ignore the fact that most black medical students have both an economic and an academic struggle. Although the few top students are wooed and aided financially by the medical schools, the majority of black medical school applicants are less well qualified than the majority of white applicants because of inferior schooling from first grade through college.

This situation has been described in an article by Dr. M. Alfred Haynes, executive director of the National Medical Association Foundation, in the AMA JOURNAL. Dr. Haynes pointed out that while we need more doctors, black and white, the need is greater for black doctors but the applicants are fewer. Many hospitals still do not give privileges to black doctors. One black doctor's wife had her first two babies at home because her well-qualified black obstetrician could give her prenatal care but was not allowed to deliver her babies in the local hospital. Another black doctor was offered a residency on the condition that if a white patient should object to his presence he would be fired. Needless to say, he did not accept the position under those conditions.

A black doctor is frequently told that he must not examine white female patients. He may stand in the room while a white doctor examines the patient and conveys the findings to him! And yet when he is offered responsibility he feels that he must accept to avoid being criticized.

The feeling of obligation to accept responsibility also applies to black doctors' wives. One told me that she was elected to an office of responsibility in an organization involved in community interests a short time after she had become a member. She would have preferred to wait a few years before taking such a position but felt that she had to accept to avoid the criticism that "they won't accept responsibility when you give it to them."

No one doctor's wife can change the world, but all of us can improve our local climate. Doctors' wives come in many colors and many widths of mind. I have never known one who wanted violence. They don't want to confront or destroy. But they can open their eyes to the problems of all other doctors' wives. And do you want to know something? I found that the wider my eyes were opened the less I could distinguish color.

93

I have stopped coloring my friends among the black doctors' wives black because what is much more obvious is how intelligent, tolerant, and attractive they are as women. I hope some day the rest of us doctors' wives will wake up color-blind.

*chapter   16*

# Stop the Committee, I Want to Get Off

Why does everyone assume that the natural habitat of a doctor's wife is the arid wasteland of committees? I have never wanted to scuttle the school system, or heckle the Sunday School Christmas play. I'm so unsubversive I even think the first of May is for May baskets. I'm perfectly willing to be vocal at town meetings, a scavenger for rummage sales, and a dutiful, if undedicated, canvasser for good causes, BUT . . . .

Wouldn't it be nice to go to a P.T.A. meeting simply to swell the attendance for your child's home room and meet the teachers you've been hearing about over the peanut-butter sandwiches without coming home a member of the Curriculum Enrichment Committee or a campaigner for cheer leaders' skirts? My next wardrobe will probably be basic tar with a miniskirt of feathers for this, but has it occurred to anyone else that the curriculum should be enriched by the faculty and that the cheer leaders' skirts might be a dandy project for the sewing class?

Once, when I endorsed a lecture by the independent candidate for senator from our state, I stirred up another batch of instant committees. Within twenty-four hours I was asked to hand out leaflets from door to door in one town, to join a bus cavalcade to a factory thirty miles away, to contribute money to the campaign, to fold pamphlets and address envelopes, and to call every newspaper in Boston to protest a scheduled debate. I hadn't planned to abandon my husband and children for the candidate. I only wanted to vote for him.

Over the years I've developed a few tricks designed to keep from getting involved. None of them works. The first attempt at evasion was to say that I didn't play bridge when the P.T.A. in South Burlington, Vermont, gave a dessert bridge. Guess who washed the dishes until midnight and closed up the gym with the janitor?

When we lived in the country I pleaded lack of time because of the animals on our farm. Who do you think was put in charge of pony rides and decorated the gym with pumpkins and cornstalks, planted and harvested by whose hands, and hauled to the school in whose car?

When we moved to a Boston suburb I vowed to wipe the slate clean. I would start fresh and beat the committee-mongers at their own game. Instead of being recruited I would volunteer my services selectively according to my own small talents. No presiding when I can't distinguish tabling a motion from recognizing the chair. No fund raising when my sales pitch usually starts out, "You probably don't want tickets to the Glee Club concert." No volunteering to sort the mail at the Medical Center when I hadn't even sorted the socks in the mending basket. Writing was my field. I would offer to write a report here for the P.T.A. leaflet, an article there for the Medical Center newsletter, and perhaps a heartwarming little piece on conservation for a nature magazine.

Well, the menu at least once a week was no surprise to my family—a casserole from the Women's Exchange topped off with Girl Scout cookies—because I was just back from an interview with the school guidance director about a series of articles, the deadline on the newsletter (of which I was reluctant coeditor) was the next day, and the galley proofs from the Audubon Society were draped all over the kitchen table.

When the girls were nearly through high school I paused one day and listened to the rattle of my brain. Why couldn't I rake the leaves, make home-made rolls, and write a story for which I might be paid ten cents a word? There I was swaying around on the back of that camel, who looked as though he had been put together by a committee, conscious of a lot of motion from side to side but very little forward progress, and I thought I was going to be sick. Also someone was breathing down my neck.

My sixteen-year-old was reading over my shoulder, adding the juicy crunch of an apple to the tap-tap of the typewriter. "If you really mean all that," she slurped, "therrsh—crunch—something you always forget to say—slurp."

I should have known better than to ask, but after shaking the pomace out of my ear, I extended my neck as usual. "What do I always forget to say?" I asked naively.

"NO! Why don't you just say you have a husband and children who like the patter of your little feet around the house? Say you have homework. Get it, Ma? Homework!"

I got it. So if you'll please stop the committee, I'd like to get off. I got so busy I nearly rode right past my own home.

*chapter* **17**

# Start Now, It's a Ten-Minute Walk to Gate Six

Doctors are compulsive travelers, not perhaps in the house staff years, but as soon as the budget will stretch beyond the supermarket. There's one place where the doctor's wife would be glad to let her fingers do the walking but it's not through the yellow pages. It's from the first set of automatic doors at the airport to wherever they have hidden your plane out back. If the airport managers are trying to prolong the contractions of our heart muscles by getting us back on our feet they are on the right track. But we ought to be dressed for it, in track shoes. Mincing along all dressed up to impress the stewardess while listing at a 45-degree angle because of the weight of a suitcase, an oversize pocketbook, and a garment bag that reaches out and hooks onto every other person whom you try to pass doesn't tone up anything but your vocabulary.

I'm not picking on any one particular airport. In fact I can think fondly of a few small ones like Lebanon, New Hampshire, or Rock Springs, Wyoming, where the plane taxies right up to a gate.

And leaning on the gate is the driver of a waiting taxi which has just planed right up to the other side of the fence.

Can you believe that on the first plane trip George and I ever took, from Boston to Newark in 1937, we stepped off the plane, walked across a grassy meadow, climbed over a fence, and hailed a bus that charged seven cents to take us to town? No more. In Stockholm, from the plane you ride what seems like an hour in a bus to the air terminal which turns out to be far out in the suburbs and then you take a taxi for another protracted ride before you get within city limits.

But I was supposed to be talking about walking. It's all very well if you are unable to walk either because both legs are in casts or because you haven't yet learned how. The airports provide wheelchairs and strollers. But if you are ablebodied and between the ages of one and one hundred you're on your own two legs. Never mind if you are carrying forty pounds of luggage, ropes, pitons, and alpenstocks. You wouldn't dare confiscate a wheelchair when you obviously are contemplating scaling the Matterhorn, and by the same show of intent you've wrecked your chances of qualifying as an infant.

In fact you've wrecked your chances of being on speaking terms with your husband. From Helsinki to Mexico City I have walked ten paces behind George, not because I have Indian blood but because he doesn't want to admit even casual acquaintance with a nut who carries gaudy paper flowers the size of parasols or a rolled up Finnish rug that I didn't think to have shipped home.

George is not the only one I embarrass. In

the Washington, D.C., airport Dr. Jack Walker pretended not to know me when I juggled a fifteen-pound Smithfield ham in addition to my other more or less normal impedimenta. Have you ever tried to carry a Smithfield ham for a mile or so? Well, these hams are longer and skinnier than the midwestern variety and swaddled up in cloth like a mummy. With the swaddling off they also look like something that has been embalmed for a long time, but they smell nicer. In fact this one was so fragrant that Jack and George were unable to lose track of me no matter how hard they tried. The only way you can carry one is in your arms like a baby. There is no handle or even a loop of string. But then what do you do with the garment bag and pocketbook even though George was carrying my suitcase because he was afraid I might hand him the ham?

Before you ask why I don't check my suitcase I'll tell you. For years George has used a carry-on bag so that he doesn't have to wait for that centrifuge to spew out his baggage at the end of the trip. So now that I often travel with him he has bought me a carry-on bag too. It is red and beautiful and made out of soft tweed fabric that seems to expand to take in all those last-minute things that are oddly shaped, like a machete or a carved reindeer from Lapland. So we don't wait for baggage. We just spend the flight recovering from the exertion of carrying our lares and penates on board. Then we build up our strength by eating and drinking everything in sight so that we can struggle two or three miles from the corrugated, red-carpeted tube that reaches out to suck one off the plane, down the echoing passageways to the main waiting room, through subterra-

*". . . .Jack and George were unable to lose track of me no matter how hard they tried."*

nean tunnels that may have a moving walkway but not necessarily in the direction you are heading, up escalator steps that flatten out before you expect them to because you can't see over your load, and out onto the sidewalk. Gasp! There you wait for a taxi for five minutes before you realize that you've got to sprint to the other end of the platform and snatch a number from the closed lips of a machine if you want to get into town before the first session of your meetings is over.

Now I realize that airports have to be enormous to accommodate all the 747s and hijackers and what looks like three cars per capita rusting away their lives in the parking lots. And I know that all those acres and acres are not to be found in cities even if London and New York gave up Kensington Gardens and Central Park. But why, when they spend millions on leviathan jetliners, can't they spend a few hundred on more of those splendid carts you can pile everything you own on and then push? A few of these treasures do exist. One of my chores when traveling is to dart my beady little eyes around hunting for one. I bless the airports where they are plentiful like Dayton or Montreal. But alas, that too is a snare and a delusion. Beware of a sudden abundance of those carts. When you see more than one ahead empty and shimmering like a mirage, you can be sure that just beyond is an escalator and you have to abandon this heavenly contraption just when you have claimed it for your own.

They do advertise little collapsible wheels on which you can pull your luggage but these devices don't collapse into nothing, you know. I am perfectly sure that if I should carry the lumpy gadget around all day, just as I paused to assemble it, a pushcart would materialize before my eyes.

In spite of the long deceptive rest periods spent in the waiting room figuring out how much you saved by buying perfume you didn't need at the duty-free store, and listening to The Voice from the ceiling enunciate Montevideo very clearly and then mumble that YOUR airline is now loading for "hasenpfeffer" at gate "ovaltine," air travel, while you are still on the ground, will soon be about as sedentary as ice hockey.

Well, a doctor's wife learns early to be resourceful, and about the only time she gets the doctor to herself is when he and she are en route to medical meetings, so neither she nor I is likely to elect to stay home. But I am looking with covetous eyes at one of those scooters the airport personnel in Copenhagen zip around on. And I think I'll add on a sidecar for all my nasty little brown paper parcels. Of course I may gradually develop stronger muscles in my right leg than in my left but that hasn't damaged the Danes' appearance. Danes are gorgeous at all ages and in both sexes. Do you think the scooters have anything to do with it or is it those open sandwiches piled high with tiny shrimp? Well, I'm for both and even if I can't get to look like a Dane in this life, my idea of travelers' heaven would be scooting along the celestial cloudways with a mouthful of Danish smorrebrod.

*chapter* *18*

# The M.D. and the Sauna

What does Finland mean to you? Paavo Nurmi, Sibelius, Iittala glassware, Marimekko fabrics, reindeer? It may vary with your age or life style, but you probably will add the sauna. And if your husband is an internist and professor of medicine like mine, the sauna will be the first on the list.

Long considered as mysterious and exotic to Americans as the Turkish bath, saunas are now beginning to be advertised along with color television and continental breakfasts to lure the cognoscente into hostelries west of the Atlantic. For $499, Messrs. Hammacher and Schlemmer will be happy to install a sauna in your home to tone up the circulation, dispel tension, and elevate your status.

So of course when we went to Finland to visit our daughter Patty, George was curious about the effect of the sauna on his own heart muscles. We were surprised to find one of these things in every home and that in apartment houses they were as common as a laundry room is here. In what we would call a garden apartment complex, on Saturday night you would see a whole family in robes, with towels over their arms, filing down the walk to the sauna. But don't confuse the sauna with a Saturday-night bath. To a Finn it is a ritual of relaxation akin to the Japanese tea ceremony in its decorum and dignity.

We were invited to use the sauna at Patty's friends' home, but because of a persistent skin problem on his feet George was reluctant to take the chance of leaving his fungi as American souvenirs. I was reluctant too, not because of moldy extremities but because I have the sort of hair that becomes instant seaweed even in humid weather. Still, George hated to leave Finland without at least trying a sauna, so he decided to go to the one at the hotel where we were staying. Patty made the arrangements in Finnish on the house phone, told George the floor and room number and pointed him towards the elevator.

George had no trouble finding the sauna suite. When he gave his name the lady in charge asked him a few questions in Finnish. He nodded vigorously, assuming that he was reassuring her that, yes, he was a guest at the hotel and he was the man whose daughter had phoned for an appointment.

He was ushered into a small dressing room, handed a robe, and the lady indicated the door to the sauna. He undressed, put on the robe, went into the sauna, hung up his robe, and sat on the bench a few minutes until his pulse was hammering in his ears.

He escaped to the anteroom, as per Patty's instructions, for a breather and then, deciding his demise was not imminent, returned for further cooking. When he fled the sauna the second time he was surprised to find a large square lady waiting for him. She crooked her finger and beckoned him to follow

*"She crooked her finger and beckoned him
to follow her."*

her. Once in an adjoining room she indicated that he should remove his robe. Now George is a modest man, unaccustomed to wandering in the nude even in his own home. Not only was the lady determined, but she was considerably bigger than he. Coquetry is not part of the role of a Finnish sauna attendant. With the dispatch of an English nanny in charge of a three-year-old, she whisked George out of the robe and placed him prone on a stretcher. There seemed no recourse short of an ignominious retreat so George resorted to the only help at his disposal. He shut his eyes!

The attendant set upon George with vigor, scrubbing his back from neck to ankles, and, with his eyes shut, he had no way of forseeing her next move. There was a moment of silence and then . . . Splash! . . . he was doused with a bucket of water that nearly floated him off the stretcher! The amazon then flipped him over on his back as neatly as a pancake and proceeded to suds him ventrally from toe to chin. He opened one eye a crack to anticipate the deluge and caught it full in the face. But through the mist he could see that she was motioning him to get up. He got up. Then she motioned him down. He started to lie down again but she shook her head violently and gestured up and down. He considered bouncing like a yo-yo but found that incredible. She definitely disapproved of his standing position but wanted his head topside. In desperation he kneeled down, wishing that he had never strayed from the familiar routine of a morning shower. Wrong again. She pulled him to his feet, sat him down on the edge of the stretcher, and proceeded to shampoo his crew cut with enough enthusiasm to uncurl Medusa's coiffure. This time his eyes were closed in self-defense as well as modesty, so . . . Splash! . . . he was half drowned again! At long last she waved him towards the door which mercifully led to a shower, his robe, and his own suddenly beloved clothes.

When his amazon turned up to bid him farewell, George proffered a tip and his only Finnish word, "kiitos," thank you. If she had knocked him flat, or slapped him on the back, which might have had the same result, he wouldn't have been surprised. But she simply lowered her eyes demurely and curtsied!

By the time George's gelatinous knees got him down to Patty and me in the hotel room, he was still lobster-red and making strange whinnying noises somewhere between laughter and tears.

"That's the sauna," Patty reassured me. "It dilates your blood vessels."

"It wasn't the HEAT that made me this red," George protested. "I'm still blushing. I haven't been that embarassed since I was in high school and tried to crash a dance by climbing in a basement window. As I hung by my fingers, I realized that I was swaying above an occupied cubicle in the girls' rest room!"

"Then why did you agree when she asked if you wanted to be scrubbed?"

"Is THAT what she asked? Now you tell me! I was trying to improve the American image by being aggreeable."

"You were," Patty snickered, looking at his rosy woebegone face. "And if you think we're laughing, imagine what she's telling the girls in the locker room upstairs about bringing the American doctor to his knees!"

*chapter*  19

# Nor Any Drop
# to Drink

From Land's End to Murmansk, Gibraltar to Lublyana, water is for external use only. It may be used for anointing, washing in moderation, swimming in or sailing upon but never, never to drink.

If you want to identify with the king in WHEN WE WERE VERY YOUNG who didn't really want to upset the royal household but he DID want a little bit of butter for his bread, just ask for a glass of water in most European restaurants.

Now oddly enough I'm not much of a water drinker at home, but I don't consider a request for it, or even the occasional urge to imbibe, abnormal behavior. Maybe it is the obstacle course one has to run before closing the fingers around a dewy goblet in Europe that whets my thirst. More likely it is the miles and miles of walking in the sun over cobblestone streets and dusty footpaths trying to absorb in a few weeks the cultural accumulation of six hundred years.

Undoubtedly there is a good sound reason for this hydrophobia prevalent among head waiters. Perhaps the local water supply was of dubious purity for so long that it became habitual to drink anything else but. This might also have been promoted by the owners of cafés and restaurants. There is no profit in a glass of water.

In one of Zurich's most elegant old-world lake-front hostelries (with prices to match), surrounded by huge trees and flower beds and staffed with hot and cold running retainers, I thought I just might dare ask for a glass of water at lunch.

"Water, madame?" the waiter asked in disbelief, glancing around nervously to see if anyone had overheard the American lady's inappropriate request.

"To drink?"

He would have been more mollified if I had said, "No, to bathe my feet," but I was determined in a mousy sort of way.

"Yes," I croaked, "Just a small glass."

"Carbonated water, mineral water?"

"No, just plain drinking water, the kind you would bring if I ordered Scotch and water."

"Oh, Scotch and water," he smiled with relief.

"No Scotch, just the water."

His face crumpled with disappointment and he fled to confer with his superior.

I could see them discussing my bizarre request with occasional glances in my direction. The captain rolled his eyes heavenward in despair and called a bus boy. The bus boy disappeared into the pantry and emerged with a silver salver and an enormous silver pitcher. Then the captain handed the pitcher to our waiter who fled to the kitchen where he must have called in the services of a water diviner. Fifteen minutes later he reappeared staggering under the weight of a full four-quart silver pitcher. The bus boy rushed to his aid with a bowl of ice and a goblet and after all was arranged tastefully on the tray it was shouldered by the bus boy and carried to George's and my table with the waiter trotting along behind to perform the final rites of pouring one glass of water and setting it before my rosy face.

This, you understand, was in the sort of dining room where fresh roses on every table and the linen was so starched that the napkins stood upright until you pried them flat and then skidded off your lap every time you moved one knee a quarter of an inch. Each table had an annex equipped with elaborate cutlery and a small burner to keep the entrées warm and to ignite the flambés and crêpes. I should have ordered pressed duck or pheasant under glass because the equipment for those was ready and the staff was willing and able.

George thought it was all very funny, but the only time I have been equally embarassed by my citizenship was in Stockholm when we saw a white Cadillac, the length of a tour bus, with white upholstery, a white telephone, artificial flowers, and a New Jersey license plate.

I drank the water under the watchful eyes of the bus boy, the waiter, the captain, and the couple at the next table who were causing no heads to turn as they picked up foot-long stalks of bleached asparagus, held them over their heads with their right hands while holding a fork underneath with their left hands in case one got away, and sucked the stalks in with gusto. In between the disappearance of each stalk they wiped the hollandaise off their mouths and stared at me to see if I was drinking water again. Perhaps they were waiting for me to turn into a frog. But all I became was convinced that I would dry up and blow back across the Atlantic like a tumbleweed before I would ever again ask for anything as exotic as, sh—sh—sh, a glass of water.

*113*

# chapter 20

# The Doctor's "Wife" May Not Be a "She"

On the staff bulletin board at a metropolitan hospital a notice was posted asking if any of the wives of the house staff could type. Underneath the notice a resident had scrawled, "No, but my husband can type fifty-five words per minute!"

Although Dr. Marjorie P. Wilson, chairman of the AAMC's Department of Institutional Development, predicts that by 1980 thirty percent of the medical school freshmen will be women, in our culture medicine has been viewed as a masculine profession.

"Why would a girl go into medicine?" is not only the most common question asked of women medical students, but it is also the title of a book, by Margaret Campbell, M.D., that is a guide for women in selecting and surviving a medical school education.

*115*

Discrimination against women in medicine has not been nearly as prevalent in western Europe as in the United States. It is an American phenomenon. In several European countries there are more women than men in both medicine and dentistry. In the future the sheer number of women doctors in the United States will probably do more to eliminate the prejudice against women in medicine than all the feminists diatribes against inequities.

In the NEW YORK TIMES of April 8, 1975, Lawrence Altman reports that a study conducted by the AAMC in Washington reveals that by 1985 thirty percent of the faculty and staff of the medical colleges, as well as students, will be women.

For years the myth that women might drop out of medical college more often or practice less than men had an adverse influence on admissions committees. But the facts are that the drop-outs are nearly equal between men and women and studies made by the pseudonymous Dr. Campbell show that women doctors practice on average forty-five hours per week; men, fifty. Women "drop out" of practice on average for a total of 4.8 years, men for 2.1. Women in the United States live an average of seven years longer than men and "thus have a longer practice potential." It has also been noted that the somewhat shorter hours that women practice reflects the fact that many are in social service jobs with fixed working hours.

A lot of women think that they are better suited than men to treat women patients. In an article, "Women in Medicine: A Dramatic Increase," by Evan Jenkins, Patsy Parker at Boston University Medical School said she was considering specializing in Ob.–Gyn. because "I will treat women in a special way and hope to give them an understanding view of their bodies and the problems they may run across."

Judy Cook at Michigan State said, "I think we need women in Ob.–Gyn. badly . . . a lot of them [doctors] are not aware of the woman patient as a woman." And regarding medicine in general, Dr. Anne Lawrence says, "This is a profession that is suited to women's personalities, the care and comforting of the miserable."

Dr. Chandler Setson, Dean of the University of Florida, shares the view that women's capacity for "compassion" would benefit medicine.

Dr. Miles Hench, Associate Dean of Administration at the Medical College of Virginia at Richmond says, "Some of the attributes women bring to medicine are much more desirable. The role model given to women in childhood is the expectation that they be more open and feeling. This can be a positive factor in medicine. The masculine characteristic of aggressiveness can be a hindrance. But neither is absolute."

What are the special problems of the women in medical school, in practice, and in marriage? Helen Loeser, Radcliffe '69, Peace Corps in West Africa, when a medical student at the University of Vermont said that some teachers still didn't take the woman in medical school seriously. They thought of her as "cute." As far as her own relationship to patients is concerned she has had no evidence that patients react negatively to a woman doctor. "They are generally overwhelmed and scared and not feeling well, so their primary interest is in whether you are filling their needs."

Women medical students and house staff officers resent the lack of facilities in housing, the locker-room jibes at women, anatomical jokes (only about female anatomy), and the inclusion of nude girlie pictures among the teaching slides. They question the fairness of an admission interview in which the woman applicant, but almost never the man, is asked how a doctor can manage a career along with marriage and a family. The assumption that all the men doctors are giving adequate time and attention to their wives and families is not valid. A male doctor's family may resent the disruption of family plans and his absence because of his long working hours yet this doctor is publicly acclaimed as "conscientious." If a mother–doctor's work alters family plans she is a "bad mother."

Can she keep all three balls in the air? Apparently the answer to this depends as much on the woman doctor's husband as on her. If her husband is traditionally raised to feel that a woman's role is child-rearing, it will be very difficult for him to change and she may elect to reduce her career demands or withdraw temporarily until the difficulties are solved in order to strengthen the marriage.

But the attitude of men is changing too. Mrs. Nancy Coalter Lathrop was married to an attorney, Vermont's Commissioner of Taxes, had two children and a home to oversee when she decided to go to medical school. She talked to Dr. David Tormey, Associate Dean for Admissions at the University of Vermont, who agreed to her plan to study on a part-time basis and arranged for her to be enrolled as a special student and thus not take up a space in the class. She is firmly convinced that it is possible for a female (or male) physician to have both a complete family life and professional career. Her husband took over willingly many of the household and child-tending duties that usually are in the housewife's province. "Without him it simply wouldn't have worked," she says, "and the children too are wonderful. They are self-reliant and see a lot of their father."

What will happen in the future? Hopefully there will be more support for the increasing number of bright young women who are choosing medicine as a career. The elimination of prejudice and put-downs, more flexible house-staff training programs (not available now in most specialties except psychiatry), improved day-care centers, and the changing role for both males and females so that a man will no longer feel unmasculine if he is expected to share household and child-rearing chores are what is needed. Then the doctor's "wife," who is a husband, will be talking, not squawking. As one forward-looking young father and husband of a doctor said, "Don't knock it till you've tried it. I'm turning into a gourmet cook. I'm a real person to my kids and I'm proud of my wife, the doctor."

*chapter*  *21*

# What Leisure Hours?

All work and no play may make jack, but, contrary to the patient's notion, doctors are not primarily interested in money. The fact is that all work and no play really does make Jack a dull boy. Most John Doe M.D.s have a stable full of hobby horses that make the average non-medical man wonder where they find time to sail, paint, refinish antiques, play the cornet, write novels, or grow orchids in the bathroom. Maybe their spare time is so limited that it becomes precious, only to be spent on things that bring true satisfaction. Obviously they are motivated both by a need to escape from the ills of mankind and to create something that is functional, beautiful, or both.

George's and my acquaintance doesn't provide a comprehensive cross section of the population, because we know more doctors than lawyers, engineers, or bankers. But here are some samples of what some of our medical friends do in their off-duty hours.

Sam P., chief of staff at a large Eastern hospital, paints water colors good enough to win in competition with professional artists. Jake J., in Syracuse, converted the whole second floor of his lake-front house into a miniature electric railroad of such scope and detail that it would never be finished. He didn't want it to be. His pleasure was in working on it, and, according to his wife, he got up at five to have a few hours with his trains before he went to the office. Sam R., a pediatrician in Florida, sails, builds a dock or a chicken house, and, when he lived in Connecticut, built an indoor swimming pool in which he swam every morning. Dan L., in Oregon, collected, studied, and transplanted Arctic flowers from the mountains to his rock garden and greenhouse. Lee P., in Chicago, is an expert at making dill pickles. John D., in Vermont, a surgeon, has made and tends a greenhouse which is also a beautiful tropical living room, in the winter ablaze with poinsettias against a backdrop of snow falling outside. Even in the city, Jim D. used to raise orchids in the properly humid atmosphere of his bathroom. David B. developed an iris garden that was a showplace every spring in Westchester. John A. is an amateur chef, creating specialties like lobster cardinale. William Carlos Williams, whose doctor son, Bill, was George's classmate at Cornell, is now better known as a poet than as a doctor except among his devoted patients along the Passaic River. Dr. Virginia A. made violins for relaxation. John B. writes not only about arthritis but also about lichens. John M. raises bees, sheep, and Morgan horses.

And if our medical friends aren't creating something with words or rhizomes or pigments, they hurl themselves into sports. Fred K. will play tennis on the hottest or coldest day of the year, but luckily lives in Denver where there aren't too many of either of these days. The editor of SKI magazine asked me why so many doctors were skiers in spite of the high incidence of compound fractures. You are more likely to find YACHTING in your doctor's waiting room than THE WALL STREET JOURNAL. George played squash in an unheated room in zero weather and guess who his partners were.

You can be sure that everyone who doesn't fall into the categories mentioned, and many who do, are golfers. Ralph S., in Vermont, was at the golf course every free minute from the last snowfall in the spring to the first one in the fall, and the fellow lining up his putt next to him was probably Dick B. In Burlington or Weston, or Mission Hills, Kansas, the membership list of any golf club reads like a medical registry.

Doctors can't talk shop at home and don't want to. Their time is too limited and uncertain to allow them to take part in many community responsibilities, and they may not want to do that either because so much of their work is, in a large sense, a community responsibility. They have got to have an absorbing interest that is completely unrelated to medicine and that can exhilarate them either in body or in spirit.

I asked one M.D. why so many doctors ride their hobby horses with such enthusiasm and he said, "It's cheaper and more fun than going to a psychiatrist and you've got something to show for it, a growing plant, a diminishing waistline, a bruise, or a picture. After all, psychiatrists are M.D.s too and we're not crazy enough to let another doctor know what nuts we are!"

*chapter* 22

# If You Can't Lick 'Em, Join 'Em

The common lament among doctors' wives is that they are widows. It is true that a doctor's time at home is fragmented. At the first jangle of the phone his nostrils dilate, he has one arm in the sleeve of his overcoat and is off like an old fire horse, sniffing for acetone instead of smoke.

There isn't much a doctor's wife can do except moan about the time he spends with his patients, or at meetings, or in the laboratory. But when she finishes the first dirge about the priority of medicine over mama, she goes into the second familiar theme.

"When he isn't at the hospital or the office, he's at that damned golf club."

It's true. A lot of doctors are addicted to the little white pill and the uphill, downhill and over-the-next-sand-trap pursuit thereof. But there is a way to prevent golf widowhood. Play it.

You won't always love it madly. It is the on-again, off-again quality that makes the game intriguing. But about the time you stop singing the blues about HIS addiction, you'll show signs of being hooked yourself.

The first time you say, "I'll never play golf again—till tomorrow," you too are on the pill marked Titleist or Royal 3.

This hot-and-cold attitude towards golf is the hallmark found on the perforated skull of every golfer. As a matter of fact, the tam-o'-shantered boys who thought up the game shortly after everyone grew bored with the Crusades couldn't take it or leave it alone five hundred years ago. The public excuse for Parliament banning golf in 1457 was that golf might replace the national sport of archery. They weren't able to enforce that law, of course, and after King James IV took up the game in 1490 they didn't even try.

Over the years some folklore about golf has been accepted as truth, which close inspection reveals to be a collection of unplayable lies.

The first example of unplayable lies is often used for the opening sentence of a golf manual: "Everyone can play golf." That must be true. I'm living proof of it, though not all at once. There are thousands of golf courses in the United States and more than two hundred million people. Now even if half the population haven't learned how to tie golf-shoe laces, or plan to sleep on Saturday morning, there could be thousands of players per golf course. A frightening thought! Of course the urgency of lawn-mowing or the rise and fall of storm windows decimates the ranks seasonally, but still golf might conceivably become, next to duck hunting, the most sedentary sport in the world.

I have nothing against sitting, except in the

dentist's chair. I'd rather sit than stand any old day. Sitting is good fun, but let's not call it golf.

Unplayable lie number two is: "Each player can set his own pace." He can set it but he might as well forget it when his pace is slowed down to four-leaf clover hunting by the chatty ladies' foursome ahead, or accelerated from the rear by a ball grazing his left ear. And in every foursome there is one player who has a compulsion to retrieve balls even when they sink into a swamp full of alligators, or his counterpart who wants to get on with the game without a second glance into the woods.

I once made the mistake of playing with George at the Greenbrier (a medical meeting, of course). Both the venerable caddy and I thought it was a terrible idea but George was hell-bent for togetherness. The day was so hot that everyone with a grain of sense was sitting with only his nose showing above the rim of the pool, or above a gin and tonic. George said that I could go at my own pace. I did. On my second shot my ball ricocheted off a rock and sailed back up onto the first tee. It was interesting. The caddy said it was a first at the Greenbrier. But it wasn't pace-setting at a club where they tee off very formally at two-minute intervals.

"Women can be better golfers than men." Now there's a heart-warming phrase for the lady who is just about to put her golf widow's weeds into the thrift-shop bag. A woman's natural advantages in this game, according to the instructive literature, are her sensitivity and flexibility.

I'll go along with the first—sensitivity. A woman is never more sensitive than when she is on the first tee. She is acutely aware of the fact that her shorts seem to have shrunk over the winter. She may laugh, but only hysterically, when, instead of the lovely "thock" of her driver connecting squarely with the ball, all that the gallery hears is a wistful "Mulligan?" as she dribbles it ten feet into a barberry bush.

She's flexible all right. At times. The wrong times. Her head won't stay down if she hears a fire siren, and her left arm belongs to Raggedy Ann when it is supposed to remain stiff. But she's inflexible about giving up hunting for a lost ball, conceding her partner a putt, or letting an impatient twosome play through.

I shot a birdie once, near the beginning of the season, when the wind was against me and I was using hand-me-down clubs. At the end of the season I got an eleven on the same hole with my own clubs. That's not flexible. That's inconsistent, and I reluctantly admit that women often are, doctors' wives not excepted.

Unplayable lie number four: "Golf is a safe sport." As doctors' wives we're committed to health, welfare, and the perpendicular position, willy-nilly, although sometimes it's pretty nilly. George is always telling me that flying is safer than driving, and I've been brainwashed long enough to believe that more people break their legs getting in and out of bathtubs than they do skiing. Golf must be healthful if so many doctors espouse it, but what's so SAFE about the game? With the golf courses crowding up, and the Commies and computers making us mad for acceleration, the chances of getting your brain concussed if you don't fall flat on your face every time someone shouts "fore" are increasing all the time. Even if you don't catch pneumonia when rain starts

*". . . .I found the position somewhat trying."*

to pour when you are about two miles from the clubhouse, a golf course is a neat place to be struck by lightning in the same storm.

Let me tell you what once happened to me in a storm. The heavens unloaded and George and I decided to make a dash for a grove of pine trees. Now I don't dash lightly with a rattling golf cart in one hand and a number five iron in the other. Somehow I tangled carts with George and my leg got between the wheels. I limped rather soggily to the pines and we both stared in fascination as a huge purple egg rose on my shin. Being a doctor as well as a bluebeard with a golf cart, my partner insisted that I get my leg up above my head. Since I never quite made the chorus at Radio City, I found the position somewhat trying. So George gallantly held my foot above my head while the rain sifted through the whispering pines and a lay twosome stared at us with a mixture of embarrassment and incredulity. The swelling and the storm finally subsided, and now I can hardly see the scar which I admire every time I risk my life in the bathtub.

"I hate the game and I'm going to give my sticks to the P.T.A. white elephant sale."

Did I say that? Of course I did, and I'll probably say it again, which only proves that even a duffer like me can be a real pro when it comes to lying. Because here I am pushing into my second half-century with no noticeable enthusiasm, about as well coordinated as a camel, with athletic prowess that has been diminishing ever since I won the junior swimming championship at Camp Ohuivo in 1926, and I can't wait until winter recedes and the skiers get off the fairways.

The old Scots were canny all right. Golf, like alcoholism, isn't a vice. It's a disease. But don't go running to your doctor with that fairway look in your eye, unless you want to revert to hearing him tell about HIS game. You took it up to escape that, and have more time with him, remember? Besides it's not all in your mind. You can't just soak it and forget it, and you won't be cured by morning.

I know that tomorrow morning I'll wake up convinced that Maeterlinck was all wrong about the habitat of the bluebird of happiness. That ringing in my ears is the call of a birdie all right, but it's not coming from the kitchen. It's somewhere out there, over the next sand trap, waiting for me at the foot of the golfer's rainbow. And guess who's going with me on this wild goose chase? My husband, the golfer. I have dates, real dates, not appointments, with my husband, the doctor—for golf!

*chapter* **23**

# It's So Nice (Rare) to Have a Man Around the House

Was I hallucinating at a recent wedding when I heard the minister ask the bride if she promised to love, honor, and open the pickle jars? Probably not. She was marrying a doctor wasn't she? If the man of the cloth wanted that knot to hold he should have included broiling the steaks, the care and feeding of animals both wild and domestic, and the care and feeding of dinner guests both before the doctor slides to home plate tardily and after he vanishes again into the night halfway through the apple pie.

The dearth of doctors' wives among the ranks of the Womens' Liberation Movement is not purely coincidental. The fact is that everything hitherto considered a man's province a doctor's wife learns to do before she has outgrown her wedding dress. Her role never was limited to dishes and diapers. It also includes putting out brush fires, castrating pigs, house painting, delivering lambs, setting up the Christmas tree, and carving the turkey. She has built-in equal opportunity to do his thing as well as hers. Most doctors' wives I know cherish the rare occasions when they are treated as the weaker sex.

I'll never forget one rainy October night in Vermont when twenty boys and girls had arrived at our house to celebrate Debbie's eleventh birthday. They were just emerging from the illusory shell of their best clothes and manners and beginning to grimace and girate normally when the phone rang and I was informed by the Bishop of Vermont, the Reverend Vedder Van Dyck, that our cocker spaniel, Ginger, had wandered into the rectory seven miles away and would I please come and pick her up right away.

Now you see if I'd been a parent with a partner in the usual sense, the partner could have driven out to Rock Point on Lake Champlain to retrieve Ginger while I manned the birthday boat. But George was not at home and in addition to the twenty young guests, Debbie and me, our census included only thirteen-year-old Patty and Barbara W., a friend of mine from Kansas who was visiting for a few days. Patty bravely volunteered to chaperone the party but Barbara, having pre-teenage children herself, paled at the thought and opted for the ride through the rainy night with me in our pick-up truck.

Of course I thought we'd be back in half an hour. I ALWAYS think I'll be back in half an hour. I'll probably think so when I head out horizontally for the cemetery. We sloshed along at thirty miles an hour with the rain sluicing down the windshield and reducing the visibility to a few feet. We left the highway and somehow I missed the right turn into the Bishop's driveway. The road narrowed and suddenly the lake loomed twenty feet in front of us, dark and ominous, lapping at the sand into which our four tires were gently sinking into immobility.

I nobly suggested to Barbara that she stay in the truck and I would walk back to the Bishop's house for help.

"Don't you dare leave me!" she croaked, leaping out of the cab before I had the key out of the ignition.

So we stumbled back up the narrow dirt road. At every rustle in the bushes, Barbara practically climbed up on my back. She's a doctor's wife too but her territorial prerogative was 1500 miles to the west and though her ancestors had come from Vermont they had migrated westward when the Green Mountains still echoed the snarl of the catamount. When we could see the welcome lights of the rectory we broke into a run and arrived panting on the doorstep to be greeted with delight by Ginger and the Bishop. I was even more delighted with the Bishop's offer of his hired man and tractor to yank the truck out of the sand.

I have nothing against a night on the beach under more favorable circumstances, but the mental picture of what might be happening at home, plus trying to drive with Ginger leaping all over the front seat, pushed my foot firmly on the gas pedal all the way home.

Because we lived in the country at that time, we gradually accreted an assortment of animals until we had one hundred chickens, twelve turkeys, four sheep, two pigs, one dog, one horse, and a varying number of cats that had been acquired as kittens. My husband was willing enough to perform the barnyard chores and far more able than I but he was working full time at the medical college and the pleasure of his company rarely coincided with the crises. Take the castration of baby pigs, for instance. I was so unnerved by that experience that it was not repeated. It never occurred to the vet that the farmer would not be in residence to lend him a hand. Being a doctor himself he might have suspected it. It was a bad morning for him all around. First the mama pig charged and sent him flying right over the side of the pen, "splat" on his face. Then after I lured Mrs. Pig into another pen, he had to make do with only me as pig grabber and dirty nurse, reluctantly holding the squealing piglets while he performed his indelicate operation.

But at least my role was only second in command. Doris M., wife of the Chairman of the Department of Obstetrics and Gynecology, became an instant midwife one early spring night when one of their prize ewes was having difficulty in lambing. John was in town at the hospital ministering to a human mama who oddly enough was in the same predicament. Doris, whose house looks like HOUSE BEAUTIFUL and whose clothes like Bergdorf Goodman, has learned to cope with bees, bulls, and the good ship HOPE. She remembered that John said to grab the ewe by the left hind leg, throw her down on her side, and pull out the lamb. But the ewe didn't acknowledge Doris as a midwife and decided she preferred natural lamb-birth. Round and round the barn they circled. It was during an early spring thaw and the barn floor was wet. At one turn the ewe veered and Doris kept on going, horizontally, face down on the slimy floor. When she finally got hold of the ewe and inserted her hand to extricate the lamb she realized that she had the rubber glove on the hand that was clutching the wool on the sheep's back. By then it was too late to quibble over sterile technique so she completed the job, not exactly with enthusiasm but with considerable surprise because it wasn't just one lamb. There were twins!

When we bumped into Dick C., Department of Surgery Chairman at another medical college, at a meeting in Nashville and asked for his wife, he said, "Oh Lucy's home painting the house, bless her!" And none of the doctors within earshot blinked an eye.

One doctor's petite wife, whose years must number nearly three score and ten, arrived late at an auxiliary coffee session and murmured, "I would have been here much sooner but I had a flat tire on the way and it took me longer than it used to to change it."

All of us laugh about these things and perhaps we're boasting a little about them too. But I'll admit it's a little harder when the man around the house turns up missing at holidays.

One Christmas we were living in a furnished apartment because we had just moved across the country and were building a house. Our belongings were in storage. I had carefully marked and kept out three cartons labeled "Christmas Decorations" so that we could celebrate Christmas with our own battered but familiar lares and penates. Our Debbie and Jim Wallman cut us a fine little tree in the Wallman's woods and I dragged out the cartons. One seemed a little heavy but I decided that must be the one with the tree holder and what our children have always called "the Jesus farm." I opened it up and stared at a collection of screwdrivers, planes, and a brace and bit! It was Christmas Eve and I had no intention of rushing downtown to buy a new holder when we had a perfectly good one, in fact two, in storage. So I found a green plastic bucket in the cleaning closet, stood the tree in it, and propped it up with a ring of cans of tomato juice for ballast. The tree still listed a bit. I thought of filling the top of the bucket with golf balls but had some doubts about George's reaction.

So I shook a bag of onions around to fill in the spaces and poured in some pebbles, that had been intended for narcissus bulbs, for good measure. The tree and I stood up proudly and I was able to keep it watered to the depth of the tomato juice cans yet below the onions lest the onions rot and overpower the fragrance of the tree. I just may never go back to conventional tree-holders. If George had been home he would have bought a new tree-holder or, if we had been in our own home, made one out of wood. But then I wouldn't have had my moment of glory which is the security blanket for every doctor's wife if she wants to live happily ever after.

I don't know where Frank Slaughter found the models for the characters in his book, DOCTORS' WIVES. I haven't seen the movie but even the book stretched my credulity. I've known doctors' wives for thirty years, East Coast, West Coast, mid-America, black and white, jaundiced and cyanotic. They don't all wear halos but they don't wear their wigs to cover horns either. I can't think of five counterparts to his useless, humorless, and frustrated ladies. Because the author is a doctor, he describes the professional background realistically but those M.D.s' wives are pure fiction. How many doctors' wives have the time, let alone the inclination, for that early-in-the-day booze, all-afternoon golf, or gossip and hot-and-cold-running hanky-panky?

Although we may moan and groan, laugh and boast about the curious chores we fall heir to when the doctor is conspicuous by his absence, what would you do if you were back again facing the minister, priest, rabbi, or justice of the peace on the day you married your doctor? Would you promise all over again to love honor and open the pickle jars? You bet you would and so would I.

# chapter 24

# Fringe Benefits

Breathes there a wife, child, or roommate of a doctor who hasn't wondered what happened to that built-in, tender, loving, medical care that was going to be one of the fringe benefits of having a doctor in the house?

It's fringe, all right. Raveled edges, that's what. And speaking of raveled edges, they must slip a little Shakespeare into the pharmacology course in medical school because every M.D.'s wife is brainwashed to believe in "sleep that knits up the ravell'd sleave of care." Your built-in doctor may use "What seems to be the problem?" for openers with his patients, but for openers and closers his family gets "Go to sleep. You'll be all right in the morning."

Sleep was quite a trick for one doctor's daughter who was given benzedrine every three hours to cure her pneumonia. Where else but in a doctor's home would benzedrine be in a sulfanilamide bottle? That couldn't happen in our house. Not when our medicine cabinet has never contained either one. The PHYSICIANS' DESK REFERENCE for drug products may weigh ten pounds but the net weight of remedies in our bathroom is a few milligrams.

When I was told, not by my husband, of course, to take Valium and Ecotrin for my aching back, I kept glancing over my shoulder to see if an FDA man was following me and I carried these concoctions into the house in a plain brown wrapper.

The dictionary says that besides being borderline and peripheral, fringe also means "subject to serious distortion due to distance, obstructions or other causes."

The "distortion due to distance" is obvious to any doctor's wife. She knows that the longest distance between two points is often the space between the doctor and his family.

The obstruction is the mote in his own eye. The doctor simply cannot see his own family's symptoms straight. He can't and shouldn't treat his family. Then why do I wince, after all these years, when, after I mention a pain at home he says, "Why haven't you told your doctor?"

I'll tell you why. Because if I tell my doctor he may leave no stone unturned, including those in my kidneys, gallbladder, and the rocks in my head. Tubes of flexible (it says in small print) metal with little lights and mirrors will start from opposite ends of my anatomy and make their slow and painful way north and south until they nearly meet midway like the Southern Pacific Railroad. I will be feasted on barium and fasted for blood sugar. Solomon in all his glory was much too wise to be arrayed in gowns made out of white paper or green glazed haircloth that recoil from contact with the human body as much as the human body recoils from contact with them.

My guilty secret is that I don't yearn for all this sophisticated medical care. I just want to stop hurting or bleeding and I'd just as soon give the assignment to a witch doctor if he would do his incantations in his own hogan and keep a doll on pins and needles instead of me. I hate filling out forms about a menstrual history which has become ancient and I feel derelict in my duty when I can't conjure up a single ancestor with diagnosed mental aberrations, diabetes, or epilepsy.

The pleasure of a day's comfortable illness, replete with pillows, hot lemonade, and books is as nostalgic as PROUST'S REMEMBRANCE OF THINGS PAST. If a young doctor's wife is in bed she is either in traction or in labor. Our daughter's hernia was supposed to go away by itself until she grew up and consulted a surgeon, at which time she went from the surgeon's office to the hospital within six hours.

I had natural childbirth not because I believed in it but because the nurses on the floor thought I was supposed to know what to do until the baby came.

As a young doctor's wife I used to feel that my symptoms lacked the charisma of those in the hospital and I resented being called a "crock" if I was observed taking my temperature. But hindsight tells me I throve on calculated neglect.

Be brave, young doctors' wives, and thankful if he leaves unwell enough alone. When he insists you are all right, the chances are you soon will be. There is something ominous about this new attention that has been accelerating my slide down the far side of fifty. On the whole, while I could use a little encouragement that a new symptom isn't necessarily the beginning of whatever is finally going to do me in, and I'm not crazy about being featured in a column called "Can This Body Be Saved?" I feel a certain nostalgia for the days of the brush-off.

So, read tea leaves, tell your symptoms to your hairdresser, fantasize about Marcus Welby, but don't limp, bleed, or groan in front of your husband. The sooner you can develop the knack of reducing your own fractured ego, the happier you'll both be. He may be a wizard to those in the waiting room but the wife he saves won't be his own.

# chapter 25

# How Now, Brown Cow?

Before this dissertation begins to resemble the small bag hanging in a Vermont attic labeled "pieces of string too short to use," let's see if these bits, tied end to end, look like a noose or a rope ladder.

"How now," I ask myself, "brown-to-gray-to-blonde cow?" After the seven lean years, and the ensuing years that were fatter but frequently full of headaches that never quite turned into chronic migraine, "What lies ahead?"

Does the life of a doctor's wife turn into a Greek tragedy so rife with suffering that her emotional experience is only the catharsis the Greeks enjoyed through Oedipus or Electra?

Is it a drawing-room comedy where everyone walks wittily and brittlely on the thin ice through which the main stream of life is darkly visible?

Or is it a soap opera leaving you with a round-eyed, opened-mouth uncertainty? Will the doctor's wife solve the riddle of life in the next program?

Not if she hasn't spread out the pieces and seen some sort of pattern evolving in this jigsaw puzzle.

It is a wise doctor's wife who learns that the recurrent other woman in her life, medicine, is not her natural enemy but an entertaining companion, never the same, always colorful like a kaleidoscope. Medicine and medical education are in a period of rapid change and evolution unprecedented in their history. The doctors and medical educators will have to look sharp if they don't want to be looked at sharply. Challenge and progress have shoved status quo back into the Latin dictionary where it belongs. It has always seemed to me that the medical approach of gathering all the possible evidence with which to pursue the diagnosis is much more exciting than the legal approach of starting with an hypothesis and then hunting for facts to support it.

You who have chosen to marry a tongue depressor, to replace the silver or tin spoons you were born with, cannot predict where you are going or when, but that would be equally true of a lawyer, merchant, or chief.

You are more likely than the average wife to achieve fame, fortune, and fulfillment because you already have a boost just by standing on his shoulders. And you can't say you never have any time alone! The next step depends on the workout you give to your natural talents. Fortune in moderation depends on the use you make of an income far above the national average. And as for fulfillment, if your physical health is a do-it-yourself project, your emotional health is even more so. The doctor's wife will never find it in dramatization of her own illnesses. The last thing a doctor wants to see at home is another patient. And self-pity for your role as the neglected one won't even entertain your bridge club

144

members. They'd rather stew in their own gastric juices. The happiest doctor's wives I know have developed interests of their own in addition to the care and feeding of husband and children and in addition to the daily round of "pick-up" work which no longer means embroidery. Now it means picking up his suit at the cleaners, picking up the Girl Scout cookies, picking up the invitations to the Ladies' Auxiliary benefit dinner, or picking up the pieces of a teenage broken romance or the loafers that the heartbroken one has just sloughed off in the living room.

I've been lucky to enjoy writing because it requires nothing more than a pencil and a pad of lined yellow paper. Unlike a ballet dancer, a writer's muscles don't atrophy without constant practice and everything from pigs to physicians are grist for the mill. But creativity is not limited to translating what you feel into words or music or paintings. Your source of satisfaction may be in baking a lemon meringue pie, and, if it is, I hope you move next door to me. Or you may place the stamp of your individuality on a Japanese garden, coaching a high school play, or making mobiles from lead and stained glass. A walk in the woods and the discovery of the first arbutus, or the flash of a cardinal's crested head may restore your wonder and delight in life. But refuel you must, because there will be times when you are stoking for two. He needs you for strength to restore his confidence in normality in the face of a never-ending stream of aberrations. You are the wife of a man who has to be part-father, part-teacher, part-God to the people who come to him for help. You're lucky to be able to spend your lifetime with someone whose finger is on the pulse of life even though it may feel like the tachycardia symphony to you. Would you want to be married to an undertaker, an astronomer, an archaeologist, or some other chap who traffics with folk who are really out of this world?

You need never worry about tiring of each other. You won't spend that much time together. The pleasure of his company will always be a surprise.

I think you're lucky and you secretly know you are smart. If you were smart enough to convince him that he wanted to marry you when you were young and foolish, you are certainly smart enough to make you both glad he did!